God Is a Trauma

God Is a Trauma
Vicarious Religion and Soul-Making

Greg Mogenson

Spring Publications, Inc.
Dallas, Texas

Published by Spring Publications, Inc.;
P.O. Box 222069; Dallas, TX 75222
Printed in the United States of America
Text printed on acid-free paper
Cover designed and produced by Bharati Bhatia
Interior art by Mary Vernon

International distributors:
Spring; Postfach; 8803 Rüschlikon; Switzerland.
Japan Spring Sha, Inc.; 12–10, 2-Chome,
Nigawa Takamaru; Takarazuka 665, Japan.
Element Books Ltd; Longmead Shaftesbury;
Dorset SP7 8PL; England.
Astam Books Pty. Ltd.; 27B Llewellyn St.;
Balmain, Sydney, N.S.W. 2041; Australia.
Libros e Imagenes; Apdo. Post 40–085;
México D.F. 06140; México.

Library of Congress Cataloging-in-Publication Data
Mogenson, Greg, 1959–
God is a trauma.

Bibliography: p.
1. Psychology, Religious. I. Title.
BL53.M57   1989   200'.1'9   89–5998
ISBN 0–88214–339–5

Contents

The Wrath of God * The Suffering God * Monotheism, Trauma, and the Failure of Calf-Making * C. S. Lewis's Theodicy of Pain * Masochism and Mysticism * Do Not Take My Name in Vain * *Sacrificium Intellectus* and the One True God * Metaphysical Conjectures * Schizoid Defenses * Don't Touch! * Incarnation and the Bomb * The Martyrdom of Táhirih

The Infectious Savior * Gnosticism * Gnostic Analysis * Trauma in Transference * Jeffrey Moussaieff Masson * Abandoning Seduction * Eucharist and Globus Hystericus * Do-It-Yourself * Romanticism * The Pleasure of Dis-carnation * Baptism * Normal Unhappiness * Dreams * Nuclear Escalation * Meaning * Deliver Us from Salvation

The Crust around the Pleasure Principle * Nietzsche's Body * Sunday Reverie * Crust-Making * Language, Crust, and Deconstruction * Death-Drive and Transference * Upside-Down * Transvaluation of All Values * Scales off Eyes

Acknowledgments

The author and publisher gratefully acknowledge permission to reprint as follows:

Section III of "Esthetique du Mal," from *The Palm at the End of the Mind: Selected Poems and a Play,* by Wallace Stevens, Vintage Books, originally published by Alfred A. Knopf, Inc. © by Holly Stevens.

Selections from *Beyond the Pleasure Principle*, by Sigmund Freud, translated and edited by James Strachey. By permission of W. W. Norton & Company, Inc. Copyright © 1961 by James Strachey. Also by permission of Sigmund Freud Copyrights Ltd., The Institute of Psycho-Analysis and the Hogarth Press, holders of the rights to *The Standard Edition of the Complete Psychological Works of Sigmund Freud.*

Excerpts from *The Problem of Pain,* by C. S. Lewis, © 1940. By permission of Collins Fount (William Collins Sons & Co. Ltd.).

The sections "The Infectious Savior" and "Romanticism" of this book, previously published in "Stepping Out of the Great Code," by Greg Mogenson, in *Voices: The Art and Science of Psychotherapy,* vol. 21, no. 3/4, Fall 1985/Winter 1986. © *Voices.* Reprinted with permission.

Introduction

This book, despite its title, is not a theology book. It is not a book about God *as* God. In identifying the two words "God" and "trauma," I wish to focus attention on the *religious dimension* of the *psychology* of those overwhelming events we describe as traumatic. When a psychologist writes of God, he must do so within the confines of his own field of inquiry, the psyche. Like Jung, who in his own way tackled themes related to the one facing us here, our references to "God" will be to the *imago dei,* the God-image or God-complex—not to God in an ontological sense.[1]

Images and fantasies of God abound in psychic life and have a determining effect on its movement, regardless of whether a God 'really exists' or not. From the standpoint of theology, a standpoint that attempts to start with God even as psychology starts with psyche, the contention that "God" is a synonym for "trauma" will seem grossly reductionistic. After all, to the theologian and the believer, God may be thought of as being in all things even as He is the creator of all things. Again, let me stress: this book is not a theology book. My aim is not to reduce theology's God to a secularized category of psychopathology but, rather, to raise the secularized term "trauma" to the immensity of the religious categories which, in the form of images, are among its guiding fictions.

Whether a divine being really exists or not, the psychological fact remains that we tend to experience traumatic events *as if* they were in some sense divine. Just as God has been described as transcendent and unknowable, a trauma is an event which transcends our capacity to experience it.[2]

Compared to the finite nature of the traumatized soul, the traumatic event seems infinite, all-powerful, and wholly other. Again, we cannot say that traumatic events literally possess these properties, but only that the traumatized soul propitiates them as if they did.

Human affliction has always been a problem for theology. Indeed, the question "How do we reconcile suffering and pain with a loving God?" has proven to be among the richest questions sustaining theological reflection. Theology's approach to the problem, of course, has been mainly in the genre of theodicy. Faithful to a benevolent conception of God, theology has attempted to justify the ways of God to age upon age of men and women who have been shattered by events which have lent the created world a malevolent cast. Barth, Tillich, C. S. Lewis, Hans Kung: theologian after theologian has attempted to minister to the interminable struggle of the soul with pain.

Despite the comparisons drawn between the analyst's couch and the priest's confessional, the difference between the two is perhaps more significant. When he examines the engagement of theology, the psychologist cannot help wondering if theology has placed the needs of the soul secondary to its own need to justify the ways of its root metaphor "God." Even those theologians who fastidiously attempt to keep themselves open to the phenomena of suffering work from an essentially closed perspective in that their thinking is committed from the outset to the service of what they already believe on instinct. For the theologian the premier psychological question—"What does the soul want?"—takes a backseat to the premier theological question "What does God demand?"

This "God first, psyche second" priority is not merely academic; it occurs, as well, in the biblical account of man's relationship with God. When we read the Bible, particularly the Old Testament, we meet a God who demands the submissive obedience of the soul to His awesome knowledge and power and who is prepared to test this obedience through torture.

Like a cat playing with a mouse, the Creator plays with His creature Job.[3] When Job enquires about God's motives in torturing him, the divine terrorist answers him out of a storm:

> Will you really annul My
>   judgement?
> Will you condemn Me
>   That you may be justified?
> Or do you have an arm
>   like God,
> And can you thunder
>   with a voice like His?
> Adorn yourself with
>   eminence and dignity;
> And clothe yourself with
>   honor and majesty.
> Pour out the overflowings
>   of your anger
> And look on everyone who
>   is proud, and make him low.
>
> (Job 40 : 8-11)

The controlling metaphor of theology is an overpowering metaphor, a metaphor that literalizes itself in terms of the God-given goodness of affliction and evil. Like Job terrified before the mightiness of God, the theologian, working from a metaphor which denies its relativity as a metaphor, must suppress the objections of his suffering soul. "Behold, I am insignificant; what can I reply to Thee?" (Job 40 : 4).

The psychological move from theology's soul-transcending God to the God-complex that stirs within the soul amounts to a Copernican revolution in our conceptualization of the traumatized soul. Psychological reflection reverses the "God first, psyche second" priority. While the theologian writing his theodicy does so with his mouth covered, ever on guard, like Job, lest his representation of suffering seem impious to his

Maker, the psychologist tries to amplify the voice of the afflicted psyche. Like Jung in his *Answer to Job*, he must write without inhibition if he is "to give expression to the shattering emotion which the unvarnished spectacle of divine savagery and ruthlessness produces in us."[4]

The theologian, of course, is as skeptical about the humanism of psychology as the psychologist is of the traumatized and traumatizing theism of the theologian. If Man were truly the measure of all things, then presumably he would be able to be the measure of his sufferings as well. But the world is bigger than Man. We exist in a creation that transcends us in every direction. If today Man's knowledge and power rival the knowledge and power which Yahweh lorded over Job, will we prove any more judicious than He in our administration of it? The countdown to the Apocalypse has now started, and it is Man the humanist whose finger is on the button, not God.

The psychologist, especially the imaginal psychologist, is not so sure. He agrees with the theologian in his criticism of humanism, but wonders if it is not, after all, a God-image that has its finger on the button. For the psychologist, Man is not the measure of soul for precisely the same reason God is not its measure. For him, both are metaphors which contain within themselves their own characteristic styles of literalizing. In order to stay psychological, psychology must take the metaphor "human" no more literally and, yet, no less seriously than it takes the metaphor "God." As James Hillman has put it:

> ... of these notions, psyche and human, psyche is the more embracing, for there is nothing of man that soul does not contain, affect, influence, or define. Soul enters into all of man and is in everything human. Human existence is psychological before it is anything else—economic, social, religious, physical. In terms of logical priority, all realities (physical, social, religious) are inferred from psychic im-

ages or fantasy productions of a psyche. In terms of empirical priority, before we are born into a physical body or a social world, the fantasy of the child-to-come is a psychic reality, influencing the "nature" of the subsequent events. But the statement that soul enters into everything human cannot be reversed. Human does not enter into all soul, nor is everything psychological human. Man exists in the midst of psyche; it is not the other way around. Therefore, soul is not confined by man, and there is much of psyche that extends beyond the nature of man. The soul has inhuman reaches.[5]

Just as psychology must distinguish its engagement from theology in order to remain psychological, it must distinguish itself from humanism as well. Although humanism and theism have recently taken to founding their identities on their prudence in not committing the errors they attribute to each other, refusing the genre of theodicy does not necessarily mean that one has chosen the genre of humanism in its stead. Despite the powerful influence of Christianity and Tertullian's declaration that the soul is naturally Christian, psychology need not crucify itself between the opposites of God and Man. The soul's sufferings cannot be divided into the despair of Christ forsaken to his humanity without remainder any more than its joys can be divided evenly into his reunion with God. The logos of the psyche, as Heraclitus wrote six centuries before Christ, resides in its own depths. When we take up the term "psyche" or "soul" as our root metaphor, a *process* of reflection—which constantly deepens itself by deliteralizing itself —begins. Psychological reflection above all knows itself, even if the reflective moment of that knowing changes it, requiring yet other reflective acts ad infinitum. Psychologically speaking, what we see and declare one moment may be re-valued and re-visioned the next, as the subjective standpoint backing our perception becomes as well the object of reflection.

Here we do well to remember Hillman's usage of the term "soul":

> By *soul* I mean . . . a perspective rather than a substance, a viewpoint toward things rather than a thing itself. This perspective is reflective; it mediates events and makes differences between ourselves and everything that happens. Between us and events, between the doer and the deed, there is a reflective moment—and soul-making means differentiating this middle ground.[6]

The terms "human" and "divine" take on soul when we see them also as perspectives. Taken "as if," they too can mediate events and make differences. Taken literally, however, they pre-empt the soul's capacity to distinguish itself from events sufficiently to experience them. On the one hand, we lose soul to the human-all-too-human and, on the other, to a God before whom one may have no other "as if" structures. Identification either way produces unconsciousness—totalized vision, white-out. When a perspective is allowed to monopolize awareness, it creates the world in its own image while remaining blind to its own stance. Like an Elohim, a Jehovah, or a Yahweh, it is utterly unable to see itself. Psychological awareness requires a context, "a perception of differences,"[7] a variety of perspectives. If we cannot say what a thing is "like," we are held in its thrall and cannot incorporate it as an experience. Jung, who was as much a therapist of Christianity as he was a therapist of the psyche, makes this point with regard to what he saw as theology's unreflective use of the term "God":

> . . . statements made about [transcendent reality] are so boundlessly varied that with the best of intentions we cannot know who is right. The denominational religions recognized this long ago and in consequence each of them claims that it is not merely a human truth but the truth

directly inspired and revealed by God. Every theologian
speaks simply of "God," by which he intends it to be un-
derstood that his "god" is *the* God. But one speaks of the
paradoxical God of the Old Testament, another of the incarnate God of Love, a third of the God who has a heavenly bride, and so on, and each criticizes the other but
never himself.[8]

A principal theme we shall pursue through the pages of this
book is the impact on the soul of monotheistic theology's no-
name God. What happens to the soul when it reflects upon its
problems in the terms of so absolute and generic a spirit?
Does it assist the soul in its soul-making? Does it help the soul
to "mediate events" and to make "differences between ourselves and everything that happens"? Or does it galvanize
those events with the numinous sheen of the unapproachably
holy? Does invoking the name of the Lord preserve the overwhelming quality of overwhelming events, embedding the
traumatic?

If "image *is* psyche,"[9] as Jung says in one of his definitions, a
God without images is a God without soul. *Whatever we cannot imagine we reify and deify.* Whatever we cannot inhabit
psychologically, we propitiate with religious responses. It is
not just that God is unknowable and unimaginable; it is that
we reach for "God" most earnestly when imagination fails
us—that is, when we, like Him, are without soul. To stand
before an event for which we have no metaphors is to stand in
the tabernacle of the Lord. Like Moses before the bush that
burned and yet was not consumed, the soul falls down prostrate before whatever it is unable to relativize into images. Just
as the image-less God of Genesis created Man in His own image and likeness, all events which are aversive to the imaginal
life of the soul have a determining effect upon it. *A main concern of soul-making is making the traumatic contingencies
of our incarnational life into soul.* Soul-making, in other

words, is not merely an *opus contra naturam,* a work against the absurd contingencies of nature; it is a work against the myopia of the spirit as well.

Failures of the imagination are not uncommon. After the miscarriage, the break-up, or the tragic car accident, we may find ourselves utterly unable to imagine our lives forward. The soul, spellbound by events which have overwhelmed it, cannot lay hold of its other images. Night after night the same dreams, the exact same scenes, return. Wounded by an event, the disabled soul is unable to make distinctions *within* the event. Consciousness atrophies. Vietnam continues as before, regardless of the fact that the boys are home. Is it not at this time, in our times of intolerable affliction, that we are most likely to reflect in terms of God? Is not a trauma of some sort, physical or otherwise, the principal background of religious conversion? When we examine closely the specifics of the events which have overwhelmed us, we find them to be the causes—efficient, material, formal and final—of our so-called first cause, God. Yes, the image-less God is an image *for us,* albeit an intolerable image. The jungle fire-fight, the early morning rape, the speeding automobile of the drunk driver— all these images may be God images if, like God, they create us in their image, after their likeness.

So long as the overwhelming event is at least slightly larger than the soul's capacity to absorb it, it will be construed as infinite. It is not just that one theologian "speaks of the paradoxical God of the Old Testament, another of the incarnate God of Love, a third of the God who has a heavenly bride," the God-image which possesses the soul can also be a severed spinal cord, an autonomous sex drive, the domineering will of an abusive parent. The AIDS virus is another example. Already a new denomination of converts trembles in its thrall. Like the image-less God, AIDS changes its genetic make-up faster than its medical priesthood can develop a vaccine. The Bible reconstellates. Sodom and Gomorrah fall once more. Deuteronomy re-writes itself in the lineage of our hematological love histories. New moralities are passed down. An Apocalypse is prophesied.

The traumatized soul, the soul that has stopped mediating events and "mak[ing] differences between [itself] and everything that happens," is a soul in need of therapy. Psychotherapy, at least as I shall be presenting the practice, consists of precisely what the roots of the word imply. First and foremost, psychotherapy is a *caring* for the *soul*. The Greek root *therapeutae* suggests "an attendant, servant, physician."[10] A therapist of the psyche is one who attends, serves, and doctors the images of the psyche, the images of the soul.

Again, the contrast between the analyst's couch and the priest's confessional stands out markedly. Unlike the priest, the psychotherapist is not in the business of *saving* souls. Indeed, from his perspective, conversion is a main symptom of traumatic disturbance. The soul, unable to mediate or differentiate events, conforms to the ordinances of an event as if it were the spirit.

Nowhere is this background to conversion more evident than in the ministries of the television evangelists. Every morning of the week, evangelical preachers invite the drug addict and the prostitute, the single mother and the sex addict to give their souls to Jesus. Pain, misery, and the wages of sin dominate these programs as if religion were unthinkable except as a balm to suffering. By the end of the show—and these programs can be showy—telephones ring off their hooks and large numbers from the studio audience, running "more like a man flying from something that he dreads than one who sought the thing he loved,"[11] hasten down to the altar in response to the preacher's call.

Watching these antics, the theologian and the sophisticated theist will quickly agree with the psychologist's critical viewpoint and hasten to mark themselves different. But still the phenomenon remains: the traumatized soul, seeking solace through conversion, gives itself over to the spirit *and ceases to be psychological.* Out of the frying pan of the event that it could not assimilate, the soul enters into the fire of a transcending spirituality that it is even less able to absorb. Like the stillness after the storm or the tranquility after the electroconvulsive therapy, a state of grace ensues. The totalized metaphor of God suffering with and for man through His crucified Son brings salvation to the soul. Like Paul, the traumatized soul now rejoices in its sufferings and does its share "on behalf of His Body (which is the church) in filling up that which is lacking in Christ's afflictions" (Col. 1 : 24). But—and here is the rub, at least as the psychologist sees it—*any metaphor which offers itself as the ultimate metaphor is no metaphor at all.* The soul's mediating function, knocked around by events it cannot relativize into images, is completely knocked out when "saved" by the metaphor that ends all metaphors: Christ as vicarious atonement.

In pointing out the grass-roots popularity of conversion, I do not intend to imply that the soul is naturally Christian. Nor do I wish to imply, following Jung, that religions are "psychotherapeutic systems."[12] My point is simply that trauma is naturally religious. The soul's functioning can be held in thrall as much by the monolithic perspectives of the spirit which would save it as by the monolithic brutalities of matter which afflict it.

Where the priest would minister to the salvation of soul, the psychotherapist would seek to restore the soul to its own activity. Therapy of the psyche involves doctoring the soul's capacity to make differences between itself and matter, on the one hand, and between itself and spirit on the other. For soul, as the Platonic psychologists have described it, is the realm between matter and spirit. Rarer than the world of matter and more embodied than the world of spirit, it is a world of images which reflect, mirror, and mediate the ways in which matter and spirit are related. What is the matter with spirit and what is the spirit of matter?—these are the questions to which the soul makes its metaphorical replies.

When the perspective of the soul is lost, we are given over to the compulsions of matter and the fanaticisms of the spirit. Fundamentalism and ideology, as if conditioned by the most primitive stimulus/response causality, replace the valuing, imagining process through which events become experiences. Like the molested child who later becomes a child molester, the traumatized soul devoutly repeats the events which have proven so transfixing for it, as if trying to recover its capacity to experience and feel.

The psychotherapist's goal is not to spirit suffering away through some secular intervention or to turn suffering into spirit—as the priest would prefer as he shepherds the afflicted soul along the Way of the Cross. The psychotherapist is on the side of *experience*. His task is to restore to the soul its capacity for experiencing events. As Hillman has written, *"Whenever treatment directly neglects the experience as such and hastens to reduce or overcome it, something is being done against the soul. For experience is the soul's one and only nourishment."*[13]

Psychotherapy heals the soul by insisting that it experience its afflictions within the discrete proportions of the images in which those afflictions reside. Neurotic suffering, as Jung said, is inauthentic suffering,[14] a suffering estranged from the images of the soul's actual life. It is in connection with this issue that religious conversion and the theology of vicarious atonement become matters of clinical concern. After two thousand years of Christian salvation, the story of Christ crucified is too often substituted for the authenticity of one's own images, despite the fact that not every wound is a crucifixion.[15] It does not even matter whether we are Christian or not. The dramaturgy of the Passion can still upstage the soul's relationship to its own images and cause it to suffer against the wrong background. Ironically, a large part of the job of psychotherapy (and a main concern of this book) is releasing the soul from the collective neurosis, which in the guise of religion sanctifies estrangement of the soul from its own images and experiences.

To conclude these introductory remarks, a few words about the format of the book are in order. Although organized into chapters, the book consists essentially of a long series of short essays, each more or less independent of the others. When one considers that a main feature of traumatic disturbances is the tendency to repeat the traumatic event again and again in diverse situations, my reason for writing a series of variations on a theme will become apparent. By writing in a style that parallels the traumatized soul's compulsion to repeat what it is unable to remember, I aim to accentuate a therapeutic possibility within the repetition compulsion itself. When a trauma has varied its theme in a sufficient number of situations, a context may coagulate around it in whose terms the event at its core can be relativized, particularized, and experienced. But in order for a trauma to break free from the spell in which it is transfixed, the imaginative process which it has unconsciously literalized into compulsive behavior must be mirrored back to it in imaginative ways.

Here, though with a contemporary twist, we are following the classical Freudian account of the utilization of compulsive repetitions in analysis. In Freud's view, a tactic of analytic technique is to interpret the patient's behavior inside and outside the therapy hour as "his way of remembering"[16] repressed material. What the patient refuses to remember in the analysis or to retrieve through free association he will behave. "The greater the resistance," writes Freud, "the more extensively will expressing in action (repetition) be substituted for recollecting."[17] By "curbing the patient's compulsion to repeat ... and turning it into a motive for remembering,"[18] the analyst "struggles with the patient to keep all the impulses which he would like to carry into action within the boundaries of the mind...."[19]

The contemporary twist we shall be giving to this account is that where Freud spoke of "remembering" or "recollecting" we shall speak of *imagining*. The psychoanalytic motto "we act out what we can't remember" becomes for us "we are determined by the literalness of events (physical, emotional, intellectual, social, etc.) which we can't imagine." Memory, or *memoria* as it was once called, is a form of imagination.[20] What it recalls into the present is always, in part, a function of the perspective currently dominating the present. Though we tend to reify history, thinking of it as what "really happened" in the past, history is not static. Inasmuch as it touches us experientially, it must enter into the imaginative modes of recollection, thereby becoming psycho-history, a history of soul. The very substance of what we remember or fail to remember changes as we, its historians, change. Even traumatic events, events which once possessed the mind and galvanized the memory, can be re-written by "keep[ing] all the impulses which [we] would like to carry into action within the boundaries" of imaginative reflection.

There is another reason for writing in the variations-on-a-theme format. In order for psychological writing to stay psychological, it must eschew the monolithic tendencies of the positivistic spirit of scientism and theology. Psychological life, like a dream series or a conversation that meanders amongst the soul's complexes, is radically discontinuous—even with itself. One theory can never encompass the soul's bounty. Soul-making is an endless process, and the events that we make into soul one day may have to be re-made the next. Writing a series of vignettes reflects that psychological writing must be as endless as the depths of the soul itself. Indeed, were we to become monolithic, were we to stop the soul's ongoing imagining activity with a final truth, we would simply be replacing the traumatic content with an equally unabsorbable didactic content. In the name of soul-making, we would then actually be contributing to vicarious religion. We would be writing doctrinal theology. Events would not be turned into experiences which lend the soul substance while at the same time allowing it to imagine on. They would be turned into dogmas, fixed meanings and psychoanalytic cult reactions.

But selling out the soul to the viewpoint of something more

literal is not the answer to the problem of alleviating the soul's distress. There is a relief that comes not from simple answers and the courage of conviction, but from increased ambivalence, complexity and, as Nietzsche taught, the courage to criticize one's own convictions. This is the soul's way. It heals by differentiating problems, by mediating and making differences within them. As Poul Anderson has said, "I have yet to see any problem, however complicated, which when looked at in the right way did not become still more complicated."[21] The psyche's way is not a way of simplicity, but of complexity; not a way of truth, but of imagination. In the writing that follows we shall be attempting to follow this way with soul.

1
The God-Trauma

The Wrath of God

When we read the Bible, we are as impressed with the dark side of God as with His light side. In Isaiah 45 : 7, the Lord describes himself as "One forming light and creating darkness, Causing well-being and creating calamity." In the fifth of the Ten Commandments, God declares himself a "jealous God" and threatens to visit "the iniquity of the fathers on the children of the third and the fourth generations" of those who break His law (Ex. 20 : 5). Again and again, as repetitiously as the throbbing of an intense pain, we are told that the Lord is "vengeful" and turns His "wrath" upon those who resist His will. When Moses failed to circumcise his son, God became enraged and attempted to kill him (Ex. 4 : 24). When Jonah shirked the call to cry against the sins of the city of Nineveh, God had him swallowed into the belly of a whale until he was terrified into submission (Jonah 1 : 17).

Even with those who had been faithful to Him, the biblical record portrays God's behavior as sadistic. Though God characterizes his servant Job as a man who more than any other has been "blameless and upright ..., fearing God and turning away from evil" (Job 1 : 8), He takes up Satan's challenge: "Does Job fear God for nothing?" (Job 1 : 9). In order to be sure that Job's faithfulness is not simply fair-weather loyalty, God and Satan conspire to test him with tribulations. A tornado is dispatched which kills Job's sons and daughters (Job 1 : 19), and he is covered with boils and sores (Job 2 : 7). Though the innocent victim of these heaven-sent afflictions, Job laments but does not cry out against his Maker (Job 16 : 12–17):

I was at ease, and He broke me asunder;
He seized me by the neck and dashed me to pieces;
He set me up as His target, His archers surround me.
He slashes open my kidneys, and does not spare;
He pours out my gall on the ground.
He breaks me with breach upon breach;
He runs upon me like a warrior.
I have sewed sackcloth upon my skin,
and have laid my strength in the dust.
My face is red with weeping, and on my eyelids is deep
darkness; although there is no violence in my hands,
and my prayer is pure.

When God, in the form of a whirlwind and storm, finally speaks to the traumatized Job, He righteously declares to him that it would be ridiculous and blasphemous to question or protest his sufferings. "Where were you," asks God, "when I laid the foundation of the earth!" (Job 38 : 4). In two long speeches God reminds Job of His omnipotent power and reproaches him for having the audacity to even faintly question his treatment. He shows Job the monsters Behemoth (Job 40 : 15) and Leviathan (Job 41 : 1) and asks him how he could dare to question his Creator when he cannot even contend with his fellow creatures.

Throughout the Old Testament, references to the might and fury of the Lord abound. In Jeremiah 45 : 4-5 the Lord says:

Behold, what I have built I am breaking down, and what I have planted I am plucking up, that is, the whole land. And do you seek great things for yourself? seek them not; For, behold, I am bringing evil upon all flesh. . . .

In Psalm 44 the psalmist laments to God:

All this has come upon us, but we have not forgotten Thee, and we have not dealt falsely with Thy covenant, our heart

has not turned back, and our steps have not deviated from
Thy way, yet Thou has crushed us in a place of jackals, and
covered us with the shadow of death. If we had forgotten
the name of our God, or extended our hands to a strange
god; ... But for Thy sake we are killed all day long; we are
considered as sheep to be slaughtered. Arouse Thyself,
why dost Thou sleep, Lord?... Why dost Thou hide Thy
face, and forget our affliction and our oppression? For our
soul has sunk down into the dust; our body cleaves to the
earth. Rise up, be our help, and redeem us for the sake of
Thy lovingkindness.

The God of the Hebrew-Christian tradition is the single
source both of affliction and lovingkindness. When the
children of Israel suffer tribulation, it is because God has
willed that it be so, and when they wish redemption from their
sufferings, it is to that same one God they must turn. To love
the Lord to His satisfaction requires that we bow down before
Him in fear, for, as the Book of Job teaches, God demands our
complete allegiance and is prepared to go to the most inhuman lengths to test it. Nowhere, it seems, are we more immediately in the presence of the Lord than when we are
wracked with pain or covered with boils. God is both the
world-destroying deluge and the rainbow which follows after
it. In His wrath He destroys us, and in His mercy He spares us
from His wrath. He is the author of both good and evil, pain
and pleasure, and of life and death. He works by earthquake
and volcano, whirlwind and storm, pestilence, famine and the
tragedies of war. His is the name we ascribe to whatever overwhelms us (lest we be accused of having other gods before
Him). His ordinances are the ordinances of trauma. His authority is the authority of trauma. All vengeance belongs to
Him, and He is in all things that seem to punish, afflict, or
spare us.
The religious moment, the moment of the deity, is the moment of tribulation or deliverance from tribulation. When the

Hebrews invoked God, they were aware of this dread paradox and appealed to His benevolent side. In Psalm 9 we are told that "The Lord also will be a refuge for the oppressed, a refuge in times of trouble." In Psalm 107, similarly, God is associated with the termination of affliction:

> Then they cried unto the Lord in their trouble, and He saved them out of their distresses. He brought them out of darkness and the shadow of death, and brake their bands in sunder. Oh that men would praise the Lord for His goodness, and for His wonderful works to the children of men! ... Whoso is wise, and will observe these things, even they shall understand the lovingkindness of the Lord. (13–15, 43)

When we read passages about the lovingkindness of the Lord, we get the distinct impression that the Psalmist "protesteth too loudly." These passages, though often clearly inspired by the joy of deliverance, just as often seem to be the propitiating reaction formations of men "that hath seen affliction by the rod of His wrath" (Lamentations 3 : 1). The story of Job gives especially clear witness to this tactic of the suffering creature to love into kindness the power which vanquishes it:

> O that Thou wouldest hide me in the grave, that Thou wouldest keep me secret, until Thy wrath be past, that Thou wouldest appoint me a set time and remember me! If a man die, shall he live again? all the days of my appointed time I will wait, till my change come. (Job 14 : 13–14)

Jeremiah invokes and propitiates God in a similar fashion:

> The Lord is my portion, saith my soul: therefore will I hope in him. The Lord is good unto them that wait for Him, to the soul that seeketh Him. It is good that a man

should both hope and quietly wait for salvation of the
Lord. . . . For the Lord will not cast off forever: But though
He cause grief, yet will He have compassion according to
the multitude of His mercies. For He doth not afflict willingly nor grieve the children of men. (Lamentations
3 : 24–26, 31–33)

The wrath of God and the kindness of God are complexly in-
terwoven. When we are crushed and broken by an overwhelming event, we experience firsthand what the ancient
Hebrews knew as the rod of His wrath. A natural piety is called
into play, a piety of terror and dread. Brought low, broken
asunder, we prostrate ourselves before the stimulus which
threatens to annihilate us as if before our Maker. Typically,
there is a moral moment. It seems we are being punished. But
what are we being punished for? What have we done to war-
rant this affliction? We search ourselves for sin. If we can find
ourselves guilty of some error or indiscretion, our suffering
will at least make sense and we can set about making our
atonement.

Often, however, we can find no sin and our affliction seems
quite senseless. But here, too, we are easily given over to piety.
As the pain increases, so too does our sense of relationship to
an omnipotent being. As the persistence of our suffering
mocks our ability to understand it within the categories of our
usual existence, our sense of relationship to a wholly other
will and purpose grows. Gradually, conversion dawns. The on-
tology of the event which traumatizes us upstages our own on-
tology. In order to survive, we enter into the route of that
which afflicts us and allow ourselves to be re-created by it.
Submitting ourselves to its epistemology, we become the
keepers of its law. "Glory, Glory, Glory, for the Lord, God, Omnipotent reigneth!" As piously as the phobic patient propitiates the eliciting stimulus of his phobia, we propitiate the
overwhelming event which has transcended us, acknowledg-

ing its holiness. Only in the eye of the storm do we feel safe. Only in those ritualized observances which the faithless call our "symptoms" are we the children of God.

The Suffering God

Whether Jesus really was the Son of God or just a man imbued by his followers with that distinction, his crucifixion at the hands of the Romans bequeathed to Western culture a wholly new concept of affliction and deity. Christ nailed to the Cross abbreviated the equation which exists between creature-suffering and the Creator-God perhaps even more succinctly than the torturous relationship between the Israelites and Yahweh in the Old Testament. Where before God had been an "anxiety object" afflicting (or delivering) man from the "outside," in the Passion of Christ God's spirit put on the flesh, crept under our skin and located itself inside our very sensations of suffering. God dying on the Cross, God dying for our sins, was God saving us through His suffering. The revolution of thought that constituted the revelation of the New Testament was that God suffers also.

If the God of the New Testament seems more kindly and compassionate toward mankind than the God of the Old Testament, this change is proportionate with the increase of Christ's sufferings at Golgotha—Place of a Skull. Affliction not only persists in the New Testament; it becomes the way to God. Nowhere, according to the logic of the crucifixion, are we more reconciled to the Lord than in Christ's Passion. By becoming a man and suffering a human death, God sanctified suffering and redeemed it. No longer did suffering punitively correct a discrepancy between God's will and man's ways, but, rather, through the agony of Christ, it accented their reconciliation.[1] As the Catholic theologian Hans Kung put it:

Nowhere did it become more clearly visible than in Jesus' life and work, suffering and death, that this God is a God for men, a God who is wholly on our side. He is not a theocratical God, creating fear, "from above," but a God friendly to men, *suffering with men,* "with us below." It is scarcely necessary to insist that we are talking here in metaphors, symbols, analogies. But what is meant is understandable enough and it is now clearer than ever that the God manifested in Jesus is not a cruel, despotic, legal-minded God, but a God encountering man as redeeming love, identifying himself in Jesus with suffering man.[2]

For the Christian, God can be known as a comfort that abides within affliction, a comfort that does not banish our sufferings, but helps them to be borne. Through the agency of the crucified Christ, suffering becomes a meeting ground between God and man. It is not just that God approaches man by identifying with his sufferings; man moves nearer to God through suffering as well. Although pain and affliction may give rise to feelings of "being forsaken by God," from the Christian perspective they can "become the point of encounter with God,"[3] the point of our greatest intimacy with Him. As Paul wrote in his second letter to the Corinthians:

Praise be to the God and Father of our Lord Jesus Christ, the Father of compassion and the God of all comfort, who comforts us in all our troubles, so that we can comfort those in any trouble with the comfort we ourselves have received from God. For just as the sufferings of Christ flow over into our lives, so also through Christ our comfort overflows. If we are distressed, it is for your comfort and salvation; if we are comforted, it is for your comfort, which produces in you patient endurance of the same sufferings we suffer. And our hope for you is firm, because we know that just as you share in our sufferings, so also you share in our comfort. (1 : 3–7)

"The Christian religion," writes Ludwig Feuerbach, "is the religion of suffering."[4] Through Christ's suffering and the mystical participation of our sufferings in his, profane man becomes Christian man. As Pascal said, "Suffering is the natural state of the Christian, just as health is that of the 'natural' man."[5]

While human suffering circumscribes the finiteness of corporeal man, Christ's crucifixion and resurrection point the way which leads through suffering to the infinity of God. "The religious individual," according to Kierkegaard, "lies fettered in the finite with the absolute conception of God present to him in human frailty."[6] The smaller and more vulnerable each of us is, the greater and more transcending God seems. His strength is a function of our weakness, even as His limitlessness can be seen as a reversal of our puniness. If we would "seek first the kingdom of God" (Matt. 6 : 33), as the scripture demands, we must surrender ourselves first to our sufferings which, by transfixing us upon the cross of our own finiteness, eventually convey us into the presence of the infinite God, who, as *deus absconditus,* is paradoxically so very present in his absence.

Theology, the logic of deity, is a logic of suffering. Above all, the story of the risen Crucified provides a model of hanging in with affliction and pain until its *logos* emerges. Though we may feel utterly forsaken in a Gethsemane of meaningless despair, eventually a meaning will declare itself if we stay with what is happening. The incredible popularity of the Christian faith resides in the soul's need for examples such as the one Jesus provides. The soul that has been traumatized by events which it cannot take in needs to be supplied with images which can bear the overwhelming events in a holding pattern until the imagination can become habituated to them. Without some kind of model of perseverance and endurance, the soul will tend to retreat from life into defensive withdrawal.

But there is a problem with the Christian model. Although the example of Christ crucified shepherds the soul through

the shadowy valley of afflicting events, it does not take the
soul through these events to *their* meanings. The Christian
model of suffering belongs to the body of Christian meaning
and returns all suffering to that body. Overwhelming events
do not have value in themselves, but only by virtue of God's
having suffered them with us and only to the extent that they
lead the soul to God. One meaning covers all events. No matter what it was that had transcended us, our suffering through
it in Christ bears witness only to God's love for man as
manifested by His sacrifice of His Son.

Here we do well to recall Nietzsche's critique of the Christian logic that would equate what is comforting to believe with
what is actually true:

> How many people still make the inference: "one could not
> stand life if there were no God!"...—consequently there
> *must* be a God...!... what presumption to decree that all
> that is necessary for my preservation must also really *be*
> *there!* As if my preservation were anything necessary.[7]

Conjuring a God who is tailor-made to meet our needs for
preservation does not help the soul to come to terms with the
traumatic events which threaten to annihilate it. Indeed, when
the soul is saved or rescued by this helpful deity, the events
which it was saved from may come to be viewed as even more
traumatic. Whatever we do not face, but gain salvation from,
remains unredeemed and becomes Satanic. Evil is the excre-
ment or waste product emitted by the salvation process itself.
Ironically, the more we are saved the more there is to be saved
from.

"No one comes to the Father but by the Son" (Matt. 11 : 27):
this statement is more than a statement of the com-passion of
Christ; it is a statement of epistemology as well. No one comes
to knowledge (i.e., the Father) except by suffering incomprehensible events with Christ through to the Christian truth that
God is love. The circularity here is noteworthy: we start with

the faith position that God manifests His love by suffering incomprehensible, overwhelming events with us and then
decree that, though God is incomprehensible and overwhelming, His one great trait is the love He makes perfect with us in
our suffering. But the irony remains that what we suffered on
Good Friday is no clearer by Easter Monday. Indeed, the
challenge of working out the unique epistemologies of what
we had been suffering then is either forgotten altogether
(repression) or attributed to the devil (splitting). By conveying
the suffering soul to the monotheistic Father (before whom no
other gods may be respected), the Christian model pre-empts
the soul from suffering events through to the particular the-
ophanies latent in them.

James Hillman has given considerable attention to a critique
of the Christ model in his writings. He reminds us that *pathos,*
the Greek root of our word "suffering," originally meant
"'something that happens,' 'experiences,' a being moved and
the capacity to be moved."[8] In Hillman's view,

> The tremendous image of Christ dominates our culture's
> relation to pathologizing. The complexity of psychopa-
> thology with its rich variety of backgrounds has been ab-
> sorbed by this one central image and been endowed with
> one main meaning: suffering. The *passio* of suffering
> Jesus—and it is as translation of Jesus' passion that "suffer-
> ing" first enters our language—is fused with all expe-
> riences of pathology.[9]

Christ's model of suffering, in other words, has become the
script for all suffering. Every event which is anomalous or
dystonic to our ego's point of view is a place of crucifixion
—abandonment (Gethsemane), agony (the whipping, the
lance, the nails), humiliation (the crown of thorns), bitterness
(the sop of vinegar), forgiveness ("Forgive them Father, they
know not what they do"), and triumph over mortification
(resurrection). As Hillman has put it,

... Christianity has nailed suffering to resurrection—first nail: it is good for you; second nail: it is isolating and heroic, and third, it always leads to a better day, Easter. Well, it doesn't—we all know that! Suffering has other models, too, like deepening in the sense of Saturn, like dissolving and letting go in the sense of Dionysus, like raging and fighting back; it can make for prophesy [sic]; it can make for love; or the kinds of suffering we see in the women in Greek drama. We need many models, besides the Christian one, to locate our psychological experiences.[10]

Nothing is more crucial to the soul-making process, the process of turning events into experiences, than precision with regard to the events in question. Hillman's move of "bypass[ing] the Christian view by stepping behind it to the Greeks, to polytheism,"[11] frees psychology to experience events more in terms of their own aboriginal or archetypal backgrounds. In the world of the ancient Greeks, a person who was ill or otherwise afflicted by transcending circumstances made a pilgrimage to Delphi and asked the oracle there *which* gods he should sacrifice to in order to get back into harmony with existence.

Sacrificing to a god within a pantheon of other gods is very different from worshiping the so-called one true God. Where the monotheistic God is at least as immense, transcending, and unabsorbable as the event His Son has saved us from, a polytheistic god, by virtue of existing in a pantheon, is a spirit of precise dimensions. Reflecting a trauma against divine backgrounds within a polytheistic context does not preserve the sense of its infinite and overwhelming proportions; rather, it divides or differentiates this "infinity" in terms of a number of gods. Each particular deity, simply by virtue of being different from the others, helps the supplicant to particularize events while at the same time acknowledging that they transcend him. When we know to which god an event belongs, we

are in a better place to individuate a relationship to it and incorporate it as an experience. But until we go to the Delphi of
a perspectival epistemology, we remain in the radical monotheism of our trauma.

The God of love has not had much love for the other gods, as
the battles between Christians and pagans attest. As John
Milton argues in his nativity ode, when Christ was born, the
oracles were stilled. No longer could Delphi give us diagnoses.
No longer could we find the altars specific to our afflictions
and concerns. The process of returning events to their archetypal dominants was expropriated by a single instance of
it, the Christian one. Incarnation, crucifixion, resurrection and
apocalypse became our model of response for all events and
happenings. The statement "No one comes to the Father but
by the Son," combined with the commandment that we have
no other "as if" perspectives before God, became the war cry
of Christian soldiering.[12] Not only did it arm the Christian
against the pagan events that threatened him with harm; it
armed him for a counter-attack. The Inquisition—the persecution of the heretics, the alchemists, and the gnostics: the
wholesale slaughter of the imagination in the name of Christian truth—reveals the shadow side of the Christian God of
love and shows us the trauma that is constellated by the blood
that washes away all sin.[13]

In the Book of Revelation, the trauma of the triumphant
Christ is made devastatingly clear. As a "wrathful Lamb" the
Christ of the Apocalypse opens the seven seals of the "Book of
Redemption," a book containing the story of man's fall
through sin and rise through Christ (Heb. 2 : 5-9), and releases
destruction upon the world in the form of war, famine, death,
earthquake, solar eclipse, and the vengeance of the Christian
martyrs (Rev. 6 : 1-17). Though Christ may be the spirit who
suffers with man and vicariously atones for man's sins, at the
end, according to Christian orthodoxy, he will also visit affliction and cruelly and despotically judge those sins.

Monotheism, Trauma, and the Failure of Calf-Making

The New Testament idea that God became incarnate in human flesh makes explicit the relationship that had always existed between what Shakespeare later referred to as "the thousand shocks which mortal flesh is heir to" and religion. Human pain had pointed to God long before Jesus suffered it. Whatever afflictions man was unable to reduce for himself became the act of a deity, the act of a god. In this way culture was engaged in a fashion helpful to the suffering individual. But when the suffering soul was unable to return its affliction to a *particular* deity, that affliction became the voice of the one true God.

The commandment of monotheism's God that man have no other gods before Him (Ex. 20 : 3) was the commandment of traumatic events which lay outside the capacity of mankind's present, cultural containers to relativize and absorb. When Moses came down from Mount Sinai, his face burned pink from the presence of the Lord, the first commandment he read to his people from the list of ten was a "divine" admonishment that they have no other gods before His trauma.

The triumph of monotheism over polytheism—a triumph mistakenly viewed by many writers as culturally progressive —was the triumph of overwhelming events over the imagination. When events defy the imagination's capacity to differentiate between them, they assault the soul as a unified, monotheistic, omnipotent presence. When the soul is unable to make differences between itself and a huge jumble of events, the soul-making process becomes crippled. As Freud and Breuer put it, ". . . any impression which the nervous system has difficulty dealing with by means of associative thinking or by motor reaction becomes a psychical trauma."[14]

Let us imagine that making the covenant with the trauma-God at Sinai was a function of simultaneously breaking it. While the biblical account holds that the children of Israel broke the covenant *after* it was given to Moses, a psychoanalytic reading of the story would reverse the sequence. Making the golden calf was a failed attempt to master overwhelming events by turning them into absorbable experiences. Unable to form an imaginative relationship with events, the children of Israel had no other recourse but to form a covenant with them. Monotheism, from this perspective, was less a triumph over polytheism than a failure of the imagination, a failure of soul-making. Man makes covenants with events in a monotheistic fashion only to the extent that they overwhelm his capacity to connect with them imaginatively—or, as Freud and Breuer said, through "associative thinking." Just as a psychic rupture precedes the phobic patient's compulsive propitiation of the aversive stimulus, a breach in the psyche precedes the making of a covenant.

The notion that a covenant with God was broken by idolatrous acts of the imagination is the pious screen memory of a consciousness identified with the trauma which the imagination failed to protect it from. Indeed, it is only after our *calf* breaks that the omnipotent God, who accuses us of breaking our covenant with Him, appears in the first place. At Sinai, the soul-making project that constituted making the golden calf was not enough to absorb the trauma which the children of Israel faced. Unable to turn the events confronting them into experiences which could be reconciled with their existence, the victims blamed themselves, repented their attempts at mastery, and threw themselves upon the mercy of the events afflicting them as upon the mercy of a jealous, wrathful God.

C. S. Lewis's Theodicy of Pain

"The great religions," writes C. S. Lewis, "were first preached, and long practiced, in a world without chloroform."[15] Affliction and suffering, Lewis rightly reminds us, have not been a discovery of modern science but were ubiquitously present in the past as well, at the time when religions were being formed. Interestingly, Lewis uses this observation to suggest that pain was *not* the stimulus that elicited religion. "At all times," he writes, "... the inference from the course of events in this world to the goodness and wisdom of God would have been equally preposterous and it was never made."[16] This statement, of course, is highly dubious. Indeed, one need only skim through the Old Testament with a psychoanalytic eye to see that the wrath of God and His lovingkindness were complexly interconnected despite their ambiguity. And, yet, as if anticipating the present thesis that "God" and trauma operate in the psyche as overlapping categories, Lewis rules out from the beginning the role of the traumatic factor in the formation of religion. Seeking, perhaps, to counter the argument of some atheists that suffering is a proof of the non-existence of God (if God be defined as all-knowing, all-powerful, and benign), Lewis declares that it is only "*after* belief in God has been accepted [that] 'theodicies' explaining, or explaining away, the miseries of life, will naturally appear...."[17]

This statement, made in the early pages of his book *The Problem of Pain,* supplies the fissure through which a deconstructive reading of his subsequent argument can be made. By ruling out the etiological significance of the phenomenon of pain in the creation of the God-concept, Lewis renders its significance stingingly present. The trauma-God that Lewis brushes away so casually is as rudimentary to his argument

—and, thus, as psychologically present in it—as the God that he goes on to affirm. Indeed, the theological sleight-of-hand which Lewis employs to defer the problem of reconciling pain with a benevolent God until after we already believe in God's benevolence can be seen as a textbook example of how defense and idealization operate in a trauma-based faith.

Before quoting some of the more flamboyant examples of this clinical syndrome from Lewis's theodicy of pain, we must note another of his sleight-of-hand moves. In the chapter "Human Pain," Lewis distinguishes between two groups of pain. The pain of group A Lewis describes as "a particular kind of sensation, probably conveyed by specialised nerve fibers, and recognisable by the patient as that kind of sensation whether he dislikes it or not (e.g., the faint ache in my limbs would be recognized as an ache even if I did not object to it.)"[18] The pain of group B Lewis describes as "any experience, whether physical or mental, which the patient dislikes."[19] Delineating the two groups of pain still more sharply, Lewis adds:

> It will be noticed that all Pains in sense A become Pains in sense B if they are raised above a certain low level of intensity, but that Pains in B sense need not be Pains in A sense. Pain in the B sense, in fact, is synonymous with "suffering", "anguish", "tribulation", "adversity", or "trouble" and it is about it that the problem of pain arises. For the rest of the book Pain will be used in the B sense and will include all types of suffering: with the A sense we have no further concern.[20]

While Lewis's move here seems aimed at more intensely focusing attention upon the kind of pain most perturbing to the reader, his motive, conscious or unconscious, is to place suffering in the arena of the likes and dislikes of a finite, ego-istic human subject so that he can later make the argument that suffering is a divine corrective of man's merely finite and egoistic human perspective.

At first glance, even the psychoanalytically minded reader may be seduced into accepting this punctuation of the problem. If neurosis is one-sidedness as Jung said,[21] and if nothing is so foreign to the ego as the symptom, as Freud believed,[22] then soul-making will require that the ego be re-made or re-imagined from the perspective of the symptoms which afflict it as Hillman has suggested.[23] The pain of group B, which Lewis's God permits man to suffer, would thus be therapeutic for man, even as, for the psychoanalyst, the ego becomes more at home in the psyche by having it out with symptoms.

If we examine Lewis's argument more closely, however, we notice that the dichotomy into which he divides pain is false; hence, the answer to the problem of pain which he proposes sorely begs the question. In agreeing with Lewis to set aside the pain which is supposedly of no further concern to human beings (A), the reader agrees as well to forget the *inhuman* face of pain and to view the pain which is of concern to human beings as if man were its measure. But pain which exceeds the "certain low level of intensity" necessary for it to become a problem to man is not necessarily *bounded* by man. The grimace which contorts the face of a body racked with pain attests to the fact that the pain has passed beyond the limit of that body's ability to measure or bear it. The cruel irony of pain, an irony which Lewis neglects to square with his loving God, is that the very increase in intensity of pain that puts pain into the soul of man puts man out of his soul.

By way of contrast, it is noteworthy to recall how Freud conceptualized pain in his theory of narcissism. In psychoanalytic jargon, Lewis's group A corresponds roughly to what Freud called primary narcissism. Wounds to primary narcissism are wounds to the most basic creature-level of our existence. Lewis's group B, in Freud's terms, would correspond to secondary narcissism. Wounds here are wounds to our sense of who we are, wounds to our self-worth and identity—wounds, in other words, to ego. From the psychoanalytic point of view, the pain in the group A sense, the wounding of primary narcissism, is much more damaging than pain in the group B sense which wounds man's egoism. It is not that wounds to primary narcissism are raised to the level of secondary narcissism when they exceed a certain intensity. From the psychoanalytic viewpoint, since primary narcissism is the foundation upon which secondary narcissism is later erected, wounds to primary narcissism will result in the collapse of secondary narcissism as well.

We simply cannot let go the problem of pain in the group A sense as brashly as Lewis does. Though there certainly is pain that is merely ego-dystonic and attributable largely to man's narrow egoism, pain that has wounded primary narcissism is basically creature-dystonic and only secondarily ego-dystonic.

Here, we must ask the question: could C. S. Lewis's God actually be dystonic stimulation which our traumatized creatureliness propitiates as wholly other and calls by the name "Thou" precisely because it is both ego-dystonic and, through the threat of annihilation, creature-dystonic?[24]

Let us now examine several of the morbid turns of argument Lewis uses to reconcile pain and suffering with the existence of an omnipotent, omniscient and loving God.

> When our ancestors referred to pains and sorrows as God's "vengeance" upon sin they were not necessarily attributing evil passions to God; they may have been recognising the good element in the idea of retribution. Until the evil man finds evil unmistakably present in his existence, in the form of pain, he is enclosed in illusion. Once pain has roused him, he knows that he is in some way or other "up against" the real universe: he either rebels (with the possibility of a clearer issue and deeper repentance at some later stage) or else makes some attempt at an adjustment, which, if pursued, will lead him to religion.[25]

Despite the fact that he had earlier argued that man seeks to give an account of the connection between God and pain only after a benevolent God is already believed in, Lewis here describes a scenario where pain has been the springboard to His recognition. In his elaboration of this point, Lewis describes this God-sent or God-permitted pain in benign terms as "God's megaphone":

> No doubt Pain as God's megaphone is a terrible instrument; it may lead to final and unrepented rebellion. But it gives the only opportunity the bad man can have for amendment. It removes the veil; it plants the flag of truth within the fortress of a rebel soul.[26]

Strategically, Lewis begins by looking at the function of pain for the bad man before he addresses the pain in the lives of those of us who do not behave in "bad" or "evil" ways. The implication so far is that God shows that He is a loving God by taking the trouble to speak through His megaphone of pain to those thick-skulled, sociopathic individuals who could hear His call in no other way. Since it is commonly believed that bad men need punishment in order to help them to become good, Lewis can most easily square pain with a loving God with reference to those cases where it is being suffered by morally reprehensible people. It is important to note here that it is as an extension of the bad man argument that Lewis, in the next paragraph, goes on to give his account of why bad things happen to good people.

> If the first and lowest operation of pain shatters the illusion that all is well, the second shatters the illusion that what we have, whether good or bad in itself, is our own and enough for us. Everyone has noticed how hard it is to turn our thoughts to God when everything is going well with us. We "have all we want" is a terrible saying when "all" does not include God. We find God an interruption.

As St Augustine says somewhere "God wants to give us something, but cannot, because our hands are full, there's nowhere for Him to put it." Or as a friend of mine said "we regard God as an airman regards his parachute; it's there for emergencies but he hopes, he'll never have to use it." No God, who has made us, knows what we are and that our happiness lies in Him. Yet we will not seek it in Him as long as He leaves us any other resort where it can even plausibly be looked for. While what we call "our own life" remains agreeable we will not surrender it to Him. What then can God do in our interests but make "our own life" less agreeable to us, and take away the plausible sources of false happiness? It is just here, where God's providence seems at first to be most cruel, that the Divine humility, the stooping down of the Highest, most deserves praise.[27]

Compared to God—who is the all-good, all-powerful, absolute truth—we, like the bad man, are all to some extent off the track. If painful events afflict us, if our worldly hopes go bankrupt or tragedy strikes one of our loved ones, God is at work, recalling us to Himself through His divine megaphone. After all, man cannot live by bread alone, and famine can be squared with the love of God by seeing it as God's attempt to lead us to His spirit which is our proper food. The things of the world are merely relative; God is eternal. By calling to us in our pain, God reminds us of this distinction, enabling us to surrender to the absolute. But from the psychoanalytic perspective, events from the so-called "merely relative" world which are traumatic and overwhelming cannot be relativized by the soul which they have punctured and seem to the soul to be no less absolute than the so-called one true God. If it is a traumatic or painful event which has conveyed the soul to a religious experience, how can we be sure whether that soul is surrendering to the ontological God of religion and theology or simply to a Superego representation which has been abstracted from the severity of the hurt itself?

At the end of this argument, it is interesting to note the ruse Lewis uses to repress a psychological reading of the relationship between pain and conversion. Rather than entertain the prospect that we defend ourselves from overwhelming events by deifying them and identifying with them (psychoanalysis calls this mode of defense "identification with the aggressor"), Lewis simply behaves this prospect.

> If God were proud He would hardly have us on such terms: but He is not proud, He stoops to conquer, He will have us even though we have shown that we prefer everything else to Him, and come to Him because there is "nothing better" now to be had. The same humility is shown by all those Divine appeals to our fears which trouble high-minded readers of scripture. It is hardly complimentary to God that we should choose Him as an alternative to Hell: yet even this He accepts.[28]

That we come to God in our pain Lewis sees as evidence of how truly great and unconditional God's love for us is. The traumatic thought that God might be identical to the very trauma we are fleeing, a thought that almost leaps off the page, is repressed by Lewis as he flees it to a now redoubled affirmation of the love of God made manifest in pain.

I cannot say whether Lewis's argument is good theology or not. It has had great popular success. It can be read, however, through psychological eyes, as a masterful enactment of the idealizing defenses involved in the deification of suffering.

Masochism and Mysticism

On a cold winter night, in what was by no means an isolated incident, a fourteenth-century Catholic monk

> shut himself up in his cell ... stripped himself naked ...
> and took his scourge with the sharp spikes, and beat
> himself on the body and on the arms and legs, till blood
> poured off him as from a man who has been cupped. One
> of the spikes of the scourge was bent crooked, like a hook,
> and whatever flesh it caught it tore off. He beat himself so
> hard that the scourge broke into three bits and the points
> flew against the wall. He stood there bleeding and gazed at
> himself. It was such a wretched sight that he was reminded
> in many ways of the appearance of the beloved Christ
> when he was fearfully beaten. Out of pity for himself he
> began to weep bitterly. And he knelt down, naked and
> covered in blood in the frosty air, and prayed to God to
> wipe out his sins from before his gentle eyes.[29]

Given the soul's natural tendency to divinize and propitiate all hurts and pains it is unable to handle through "associative thinking or motor reaction," we should not be surprised to find masochistic suffering playing a central role in the lives of persons who have intentionally sought encounters with God. In order to enhance their relationship to God, mystics, saints, and martyrs have long exploited the physiological relationship between suffering and spirituality by intentionally subjecting themselves to pain and affliction. Just as the divinely victimized Job shrieked out in his torments, "Even after my skin is destroyed, Yet from my flesh I shall see God" (Job 19 : 26), many religious seekers have attempted to awaken the gift of mystic vision in themselves by deliberately destroying their flesh through self-mortifying acts.

The more we are hurt, the more we are beside ourselves with pain, the closer we are to ecstatic union with that overwhelming intensity of stimulus the pious have called God. While low levels of pain may make us peevish and personal, intolerable affliction destroys the self, releasing the sufferer from the finite limits personhood had imposed. As Karen

Horney writes, ". . . all masochistic strivings are ultimately directed toward satisfaction, namely, toward the goal of oblivion, of getting rid of self with all its conflicts and all its limitations."[30]

In the annihilation of the soul's capacity to make experiences, the mystic "experiences" divine rapture. As the intensity of a pain grows greater and greater, it eventually surpasses the capacity of the imagination to accommodate it.[31] Consciousness atrophies. Metaphors give way to symbols. Held in thrall by the flaming nerves that burn in the tortured body, the traumatized soul surrenders its imaginal freedom and prostrates itself before the fire of the body's agony as before a vision of the Lord. What had begun simply enough as the painful sensations of self-torture becomes in an instant —precisely that instant in which the agony is intensive enough to estrange the soul from the body—the symbolism of a transcending spirituality. "I could not possibly explain it," writes St. Theresa of Avila:

> In his hands I saw a great golden spear, and at the iron tip there appeared to be a point of fire. This he plunged into my heart several times so that it penetrated to my entrails. When he pulled it out, I felt that he took them with it, and left me utterly consumed by the great love of God. The pain was so severe that it made me utter several moans. The sweetness caused by this intense pain is so extreme that one cannot possibly wish it to cease, nor is one's soul then content with anything but God.[32]

The way of the mystic is the way of affliction. By inflicting pain upon herself, the mystic intensifies the "profound disharmony between the sense-world and the human self"[33] until the physical world feels completely inhospitable and her desirous body "creates/From its own wreck the thing it contemplates. . . ."

Although the New Testament does not specifically instruct the Christian soul to torture itself, it states quite clearly that the path of the Christian is a path that leads through suffering. "Through many tribulations," the Apostles told new initiates, "we must enter the kingdom of God" (Acts 24 : 22). "Behold," Jesus told his followers, "I have given you authority to tread upon serpents and scorpions . . . nothing will hurt you" (Luke 10 : 19). Paul is particularly clear on this point, "boasting" of his own afflictions (2 Cor. 11 : 23–33) as if these were the humbling prerequisites to the "visions and revelations of the Lord" he had been subject to (2 Cor. 12 : 1–10). In the same passage Paul tells his Corinthian audience that he suffered "a thorn in the flesh, a messenger of Satan to buffet me—to keep me from exalting myself" because of "the surpassing greatness of the revelations." Despite three appeals to God for healing, Paul writes, his malady persisted. Nevertheless, the great apostle suffered his thorn gladly, for the Lord told him, "My grace is sufficient for you, for power is perfected in weakness."

Just as crucifixion was followed by resurrection in the life of Christ, the mystic attempts to partake in the pleasures of Christ's risen life by following "the Way of the Cross" through whatever sorrows and humiliations he can subject himself to.[34] As the fourteenth-century mystic John Tauler explains in his "Second Sermon for Easter Day":

> A great life makes reply to him who dies in earnest even in the least of things, a life which strengthens him immediately to die a greater death; a death so long and strong, that it seems to him hereafter more joyful, good and pleasant to die than to live, for he finds life in death and light shining in darkness.[35]

Suffering, in the words of Thomas à Kempis, author of the classic text of Catholic devotion *De Imitatione Christi*, is the "gymnastic of eternity," the "terrible initiative caress of God."

While mostly the soul flees pain as if it were fleeing the wrath of God, it can also deify traumatic stimulation by willingly impaling itself upon it like the saints, mystics and martyrs who run so "eagerly and merrily to the Cross." Just as God is encountered in pestilence and death, famine and flood, earthquake and lightning flash, He is encountered as well in the sting of the scourge with which one assaults one's own body. Through acts of masochism, the seeker of God can invoke the loving sadism of his Lord's touch. Marx was right: religion *is* the opium of the people. With the same firing of nervous impulses that the flagellant invokes God, he releases the natural opiates in his afflicted body. God is the leather strap, the willow switch, the cat-o'-nine-tails, and the cane. He is the gnashing of the teeth, the raving of the nerves, and the creature's anguished cry. No matter how we are flayed, cut, broken, or pierced—voluntarily or involuntarily—we encounter God in trauma.

Do Not Take My Name in Vain

In his book *The Idea of the Holy*, Rudolf Otto speculates that the earliest names for deity were derived from the inarticulate shrieks and cries which were emitted from the larynx of early man when he shuddered in terror and amazement before overwhelmingly numinous events. Quoting from the Kena-Upanishad, Otto shows how involuntary sounds that express the numinous feelings stirring in man when he encounters overwhelming events (e.g., lightning) may have become associated with the Numinous itself:

> This is the way It (*sc.* Brahman) is to be illustrated:
> When the lightnings have been loosened:
>   Aaah!

When that has made the eyes be closed—
  Aaah!—
So far concerning Deity (*devata*).[36]

If Otto is correct, if the earliest names man gave to deity cor-
responded to the gasps and cries of his startled, frightened
creaturehood, the commandment that we not take the name
of the Lord in vain (Ex. 20 : 7) is tantamount to a commandment that we cover our mouths, split off our reactions to what
has hurt or frightened us, and reverence it with silence.

I flailed my fists at nothing,
And yet I was defeated.
My soul of itself did tire,
And I longed for the dust to claim me.
But when a groan interrupted my dying,
I glimpsed a strange justice dependent upon
The merciless turning of the world.[37]

When the soul tires of itself and words fail, when metaphors
can no longer be found through which to individuate a relationship to transcending events, a groan may be emitted, a
groan so split off from the soul's usual experience of itself that,
as Paul would later say, it seems to be "not I who speak, but
Him in me." By prohibiting the invectives of the traumatized
soul, the commandment not to take the name of the Lord in
vain deprives it of its most natural mechanism for anxiety
release. Presumably, if we could utter a shriek or a moan these
could be used to differentiate overwhelming experiences at
least to a minimal degree. Were the soul permitted to hear the
difference between one groan and another, the differences in
intensity, pitch and timbre, it could use these sounds as metaphors to particularize the events which overwhelm it. But the
commandment not to cry out forbids the comparison of inarticulate sounds, preserving the awesomeness of the eliciting
stimulus and traumatic response. With each cry that is held

back in the throat, the event to which it was a response becomes more and more other until, like a God, it becomes wholly other. God is the deferral of cursing and swearing, the deferral of groaning, weeping, howling and shrieking, and the indefinite postponement of whimpering in the dark. He is the inarticulate made Holy, the sanctification of the literally unspeakable, a circumcised tongue.

Of course, the commandment not to take the name of the Lord in vain is also a commandment not to swear false covenants. When men made covenants or contracts with one another, they solemnized them by swearing before the presence of God. "If I default on my agreement with you, may the Lord strike me dead with lightning." Ironically, the overwhelming events with which early man made covenants in order to render them less traumatic and less unpredictable became the background in whose terms he attempted to render his secular affairs more benign and predictable. Agreements made with reference to the name of God were made with reference to that jumble of traumatic events before which man trembled when he uttered the inarticulate sounds from which the deity's name was later derived. God is as severe as the events that took our speech away, replacing it with the cries and groans of a traumatized creaturehood. "If I break my agreement with you, may God subject me to the moaning and groaning of the sufferings which mankind has attempted to propitiate by splitting off and deifying."

Words, as the saying goes, are cheap. In order to make them binding and substantive, early man linked them to the inarticulate shrieks and moans through which he submitted to the authority of overwhelming stimulation as if before a God. Even today, words may seem more credible if there is a plaintiveness in them, an inarticulate excess of emotion. And, yet, like a confession at gun-point, trauma-laden speech may give us cause for skepticism. Its sincerity may be entirely a function of its identification with the power that has transcended, hurt, startled or frightened it.

In the New Testament, Jesus, God's suffering son, is called "the Word" and described as being linguistically pre-existent in God. "In the beginning there was the Word, and the Word was with God, and the Word was God" (John 1 : 1). Perhaps, this Christic-Word which dwelt from the beginning with God and which later "became flesh" (John 1 : 14) was actually the pathetic groan or inarticulate whimper of early man—not a word at all but, rather, the failure of words, an anti-word: No one comes to the Father but by the shrieks and groans of His Son, the "living Word." Christ groaning on the cross, Christ groaning *with* us, is Christ groaning vicariously *for* us.

If, as T. S. Eliot wrote, the world will end "not with a bang but a whimper," perhaps it will be with the whimpers we have "given to the Lord." If, today, "we are hollow men," perhaps it is because throughout our yesterdays we have devalued ourselves through monotheism. After several millennia of our endowing overwhelming events with the incarnational vulnerability which they make so unbearable in ourselves, the whimpering of our displaced humanity has probably reached the mega-tonnage sufficient to break forth with quite a bang. On the other hand, if each of us, individually, would allow ourselves to whimper—to whimper and curse, and curse and swear—perhaps we could begin to diffuse the stockpile of insufficiently experienced events and emotions that we have given to the Lord and learned to call God.

Sacrificium Intellectus and the One True God

"If God is small enough for me to understand Him, then He's not big enough to be God!" says the believer with a blink. Perhaps no popular adage could better express how the no-name God of monotheistic religion produces unconsciousness. The adage not only displays a mind-set for which the will to believe has upstaged the will to understand, it displays a predilection for believing *big*. "If you're going to believe, believe BIG!" booms the believer in a big voice. Ironically, while monotheistic religion boasts that its God is larger than what its understanding can encompass, His size does not exceed the immensity of the credulity it demonstrates with this boasting. Perhaps large monotheistic Gods are not exclusively the consequence of huge tribulations, but are the consequence of big believers as well. Indeed, what would become of the one true God, the jealous God before whom one may recognize no other categories of understanding, if He did not have big believers to sustain and promote Him?

Traumatic events are not all painful. Frequently, the imagination is fixated by events which stop it from imagining on, but which do not cause pain. The birth of a child, for instance, may be as overwhelming for the new father as for the mother. The sudden appearance of the new life immediately cancels the conventions of its parents' old life, temporarily bankrupting their previous soul-making. We should not be surprised, therefore, that new parents often claim to be afraid of their children and sometimes even suffer depression or psychosis following a birth they may have joyously anticipated. It is a tremendous responsibility to be the parent of an overwhelming event, the mother of God.

But even events that are neither painful nor as overwhelming as the "miracle of childbirth" can stop the imagination when they are taken to be subject to the will of a divine being whom by definition we cannot understand. If God would not be God if he were small enough for man to understand, and if God is working in mysterious ways in events that defy man's comprehension, it would be hubris for men and women to try to bring clarity to life through the action of their own minds. The more we hold to be accounted for by an explanatory category which we do not understand, the more we fail to grapple with the mystery of the events themselves. The idea that God is absolutely beyond man's capacity to fathom dislocates the mediating function of the imagination, devaluing the metaphors and models it creates as merely the productions of a finite intelligence. But when the soul-making process is devalued, the psyche itself is at risk. The soul-destroying consequence of worshiping a God who is identical with our inability to understand Him is that we tend to propitiate, as if they too were completely transcending, events which the soul might easily comprehend and absorb.

It is not only as the defensive maneuver of an exhausted imagination that the God-concept appears and produces unconsciousness. Unconsciousness is built right into the notion of an omniscient God. Inasmuch as we "explain" what we cannot understand by dropping the name of a God we hold to be at least as inexplicable, we have merely glorified darkness as mystery. The unfathomable mind of God is an anti-concept which clarifies nothing. It is not just that the less we can explain the more omniscient we believe God to be. The corollary is also true: the more omniscient God seems to be, the less we even attempt to make comprehensible for ourselves.

What happens to events when we try to come to terms with them by appealing to the God whose claim to divinity resides in His being bigger than what we can understand? More: what happens to our *relationship* with events we cannot yet comprehend when we attempt to comprehend them in terms of a God whose omniscience is a function of the *sacrificium intellectus* we make when turning to Him?

Even when we leave quite to one side references to the wrath of God and stress, as does our loud believer, that He works in mysterious ways which are ultimately loving and benign, the God-concept can have a traumatizing effect on the psyche. *Whenever the core category of our epistemology is a divine category whose ways are inscrutable and mysterious, the overwhelming quality of the events we refer to it is preserved.* The less we can make sense of our world, the more omniscient God seems. The more unable we are to make a residence for ourselves in the world, the more we seem to rest in Him.

The God before whom one may have no other forms of knowing is a disturbed metaphor. While it moves in the psyche among other metaphors, it is a metaphor that denies its relativity as a metaphor. Obsessive-compulsive, monomaniacal, paranoid: the monotheistic God-image is the presiding deity over many clinical syndromes. In order to remain psychological, the psyche must not only relativize the material and social events that overwhelm it, but the ideological and religious ones as well. And, of course, first among these is the One who must always be first, the One who commands us to know Him as the one true God.

Metaphysical Conjectures

"God is a conjecture," wrote Nietzsche in *Zarathustra*, "but I desire that your conjectures should not reach beyond your creating will."[38] In Nietzsche's view, it is decadent to worship a metaphysical object, an object that is beyond the scope of the culture which we as culture-makers are creating. To do so is only to worship a projected, reified, hypostatized version of the existential issues we have been unable to confront and absorb. The Creator-god which men conjecture is inversely proportionate to their creative responses to the challenges of existence. The paler a people's response, the more bloated has become their God with projected creativity. By declaring the death of God, Nietzsche sought to release again into human hands the creative power that man had displaced into the Godhead. God, in Nietzsche's view, did not make Adam out of clay during the second week of an original creation; rather, men fashioned God out of clay, erased their fingerprints, and then blew the graven idol into supernatural proportions by means of abnegations of the will.

But why is man so quick to hide his creative power in a metaphysical conjecture, a metaphysical conceit? Perhaps it is because Necessity, the mother of invention, is not appeased by our creative efforts, but again and again snarls our path with obstacles and troubles. While civilization has solved many human problems, there are other problems which have proved insoluble. As Shelley put it in *Prometheus Unbound,* if it were not for the "clogs" of "chance, and death, and mutability," the imagination of man "might oversoar / The loftiest star of unascended heaven, / Pinnacled dim in the intense inane." Unable to exhaust the contingencies that drive us to create with our inventions, we eventually abdicate our creative power and reside conflict-free in the state of grace that accompanies the projection of our creative power, the abnegation of our will. But residing in grace is like living on credit. Sooner or later our account comes due, and we find ourselves irredeemably overdrawn. So bankrupt have we become by the worship of our old God that we require a new God to bail us out.

Just as we conjecture a creation to end all creation, a God to end all Gods, now we require a sacrifice to end all sacrifice. We require a vicarious atonement, a new testament to balance the vicarious displacements of the old testament. Unable to create our way out or through the traumatic level of existence, we conjecture a way out beyond the reach of our creating will. When this also breaks down and the trauma ("chance, and death, and mutability") confronts us again, we try to patch up the cracks in our theological defenses by packing the trauma off on the scapegoat's back with the notion of an only begotten Son who takes the sins and pains of the world onto his shoulders and suffers them all for us.

Schizoid Defenses

Trauma is the body of the world and the body of man. "Chance, and death, and mutability" are our existential lot. To defend himself from the ontological insecurity of existence, man has developed schizoid defenses. To use Laing's terminology, the self has been divided. The self splits off from the body and hovers above it—a false self. World becomes mere worldliness, and a transcendental, heavenly world is split off and affirmed.

> The self, as long as it is "uncommitted to the objective element", is free to dream and imagine anything. Without reference to the objective element it can be all things to itself—it has unconditioned freedom, power, creativity. But its freedom and its omnipotence are exercised in a vacuum and its creativity is only the capacity to produce phantoms. The *inner honesty, freedom, omnipotence,* and *creativity,* which the "inner" self cherishes as its ideals, are cancelled, therefore, by a co-existing tortured sense of self-duplicity, of the lack of any real freedom, of utter impotence and sterility.[39]

As the self grows bigger and bigger in its disembodied vacuum, as God grows bigger and bigger in his world-transcending vacuum, larger and larger traumatic experiences are required to bring the consciousness that has split off into the false-self and God back into touch with the body of the world and man. The traumatic events we deny return to us cumulatively. At the end of millennia, there are indeed judgment days, days of reckoning. The bigger God becomes, the more events we channel off into the void of his righteousness, love, and grace, the more perilous becomes the human situation. And God does become bigger:

> The schizoid defense against "reality" has, however, the grave disadvantage that it tends to perpetuate and potentiate the original threatening quality of reality.[40]

Mountains get made out of avoided molehills, and then,

ironically, the molehills of a millennium of denial *do* sum up to mountains. In order for us to feel anything in our aloof vacuum, there must be huge explosions. In order to break through our catatonic withdrawal, there must be shock treatments. When man created God he created the Auschwitz oven. The flaming fire-pot that Abraham saw in his dream of the ceremony of the covenant with Yahweh returns in the demonic guise of Hitler's final solution. In order for us to feel anything, six million people had to be exterminated. This century has enacted a Derridean deconstruction of our civilization's logo-centric, Judeo-Christian defense—the Judeo-Christian covenant. In the text of history we can read the subtext of God, the horror of the Great Code. God is the oven. God is the atom bomb. God is a trauma.

Don't Touch!

The finger burned on the hot stove supplies the decision to avoid the repetition of a similar event in the future. "Once burned, twice shy" goes the popular adage. The relationship that develops between the singed finger and the aversive object—in this case the kitchen stove—is based upon mistrust. The burned finger comes to respect the hot stove, to reverence and propitiate it. The reflex withdrawing the burned finger, the finger's pained response, is an act of piety before the glowing element, an act of prostration before the stimulus, the stove. Pentecost: recoiling from its experience of the stove-god, the finger stiffens and throbs, slayed in the spirit. Prayers are offered; devotions are observed; oven-mitts and priestly robes are worn. In the rhetoric of trust, supplications are made to the object of our mistrust: "Lord have mercy upon us." "Forgive us our trespasses." "Lead us not into temptation [trauma], but deliver us from evil [pain]." In order to protect ourselves from what has hurt us, we whitewash it and identify with it. Our trauma is converted into a loving father, and our mistrust is refined into a covenantal relationship with Him. Religion originates at our finger tips.

Incarnation and the Bomb

What is pathological about incarnational thinking is that it is exaggerated in two directions at once. Both in its idealism and in its pragmatism it goes too far. The incarnational mind imagines in terms of ultimate inventions and final solutions. Its logic is a logic of God becoming man and of man becoming God. Its fascination is with a sacrifice to end all sacrifice, a "once and for all" solution. What the incarnational perspective reckons to be spirit it must render in the flesh. The proof is in the pudding. Just ask the Japanese. They have become experts on incarnation—American-pragmatist style. They study it, replicate it, and industrialize it, because they are fixated in the trauma of it. (Identification with the aggressor is the specific defense mechanism.) The Americans so loved the world and peace that they nuked the Japanese for its redemption. Truman justified the atomic bomb as the necessary violence in a war that would end all war. No more pistols and grenades. No more eye for an eye, tooth for a tooth, Old Testament combat. It's the New Testament now. Now we will call into being a new order. Now we will destroy whole cities with our Savior-bombs. After all, isn't that the mystery: they have to lose their lives to gain them, in a higher form, redeemed?

The Martyrdom of Táhirih

God is a trauma, the sum of the pains, problems and catastrophes we have been unable to absorb into creative responses. The name "God" is the X value we assign to events that are too hot to handle, too big, too numinous, too unknown. Religion, likewise, is a form of divine arithmetic, an algebra of propitiation.

The end of religion, theoretically, would correspond to the absorption of its traumatic contents and iconographic substitutes into man's ongoing creative process, into soul. At the apocalyptic end of a millennium, the trauma which has been displaced into the extra-human world of spiritual conjectures erupts. We pass beyond our eschatology, beyond our conjectures, beyond the orienting structures of our fear. The world comes to an end. Usually, this ending is conceived of moralistically as a judgment day. On the one hand, a trauma-free heaven is imagined for those who have piously propitiated the trauma; on the other hand, a traumatic hell is imagined for those who have not worshiped the trauma. Clearly, this moralistic mythology of the final absorption of trauma is the expression of a consciousness still very much engaged in propitiating trauma.

In the Book of Revelation, the triumphant assimilation of trauma is imagined as the marriage of Christ and the city, New Jerusalem, which descends out of heaven as a Bride adorned to meet the Bridegroom. In this marriage the incest taboo is finally lifted, and we are to enter a new dispensation, one entirely different from the Old Testament totem and taboo.

In our culture, in most cultures, women have been associated with what Jung called "earth, darkness, the abysmal side of the bodily man with his animal passions and instinctual nature and to 'matter' in general."[41] While men have tended to be regarded as rational spirits, women have tended to be seen as irrational, inferior, and weak. Whether as Lilith, Eve, Pandora, Whore of Babylon, witch at the stake or hysteric in Charcot's clinic, woman has been imagined to be either trauma itself or particularly susceptible to it.

Like everything else that is associated with trauma, woman is split in two. Just as we conjecture about traumatic events in terms of pain and pleasure, good and bad, positive and negative, heaven and hell, we split the feminine into a virgin and a whore. Whether we look east to the Arab countries where women are covered from head to toe or west to America where women are more scantily clad, the whore-madonna complex is everywhere present.

But what does all this look like at the end of a millennium of prohibitions and propitiations? What does it look like when the traumatic contents of a culture shed the trappings of misogynist repression and stand before the culture as a bride before her husband?

In 1850, in the Persian hamlet of Badasht, Bahá'u'lláh, prophet and founding father of the Bahá'í religion, gathered eighty-one followers around him and revealed to them daily a new dispensation from the old Islamic law.

> Each day of that memorable gathering witnessed the abrogation of a new law and the repudiation of a long-established tradition. The veils that guarded the sanctity of the ordinances of Islam were sternly rent asunder, and the idols that had so long claimed the adoration of their blind worshippers were rudely demolished.[42]

The conference at Badasht was similar in a sense to Christ's Sermon on the Mount. Bahá'u'lláh's daily abrogation of a traditional Islamic law was intended to inaugurate a new aeon even as Christ sought to inaugurate a new aeon by giving the old Jewish laws a new twist: "You have heard that the ancients were told. . . . But I say unto you that. . . ." Bahá'u'lláh doubtless saw his law-breaking as the fulfillment of the orthodox tradition. Like Christ, he had not come "to abolish the Law or the Prophets but to fulfill [them]."

The key difference between the Sermon on the Mount and the conference at Badasht was that, while Christ's revision of the Law was given to prepare man for the *coming* of the end of the world and the Kingdom of God, Bahá'u'lláh's lawbreaking was an attempt to help man to take up residence in a world which had already ended, a kingdom that had already come. If the situation during Christ's time was pre-apocalyptic (as presumably it still is for the Judeo-Christian world), the situation for the followers of Bahá'u'lláh was apocalyptic right at the very time of the Badasht conference. Perhaps what happened next at Badasht can be accounted for in terms of the apocalyptic intensity with which the conference was invested, a traumatic intensity for which not everyone present was ready.

During the conference, the famous female follower of Bahá'u'lláh, Táhirih, was reproached by her more conservative fellow-disciples for transgressing the time-honored traditions of Islamic law. The issue came to a head when Táhirih appeared before her fellow-disciples unveiled.

> Consternation immediately seized the entire gathering. All stood aghast before this sudden and most unexpected apparition. To behold her face unveiled was to them inconceivable. Even to gaze at her shadow was a thing which they deemed improper, inasmuch as they regarded her as the very incarnation of Fátimih [the daughter of Muhammad], the noblest emblem of chastity in their eyes.
>
> Quietly, silently, and with the utmost dignity, Táhirih stepped forward and, advancing towards Quddús, seated herself on his right-hand side. Her unruffled serenity sharply contrasted with the affrighted countenances of those who were gazing upon her face. Fear, anger, and bewilderment stirred the depths of their souls. That sudden revelation seemed to have stunned their faculties. 'Abdu'l-Kháliq-i-Lsfáhani was so gravely shaken that he cut his throat with his own hands. Covered with blood and shrieking with excitement, he fled from the face of Táhirih. A few, following his example, abandoned their companions and forsook their Faith. A number were seen standing speechless before her, confounded with wonder.... A feel-

ing of joy and triumph had now illumined her face. She rose from her seat and, undeterred by the tumult that she had raised in the heart of her companions, began to address the remnant of that assembly. Without the least premeditation, and in language that bore a striking resemblance to that of the Qur'án, she delivered her appeal with matchless eloquence and profound fervor. She concluded her address with this verse of the Qur'án: "Verily, amid gardens and rivers shall the pious dwell in the seat of truth, in the presence of the potent King." . . . [Concluding her address, Táhirih declared:] "This day is the day of festivity and universal rejoicing," [. . .] "the day on which the fetters of the past are burst asunder. Let those who have shared in this great achievement arise and embrace each other."[43]

Unfortunately, the trauma that was released with the unveiling of Táhirih's face was not absorbed into her eloquent assurances. Following the Badasht conference were years of persecution and martyrdom. Thousands of Bahá'í were put to death in the cruelest ways imaginable (as they are to this day).

By the testimony of Bahá'u'lláh, that heroic youth [Quddús], was subjected to such tortures and suffered such a death as even Jesus had not faced in the hour of His greatest agony. The absence of any restraint on the part of the government authorities, the ingenious barbarity which the torture-mongers of Bárfurúsh so ably displayed, and fierce fanaticism which glowed in the breasts of its shi'ah inhabitants, the moral support accorded to them by the dignitaries of Church and State in the capital—above all, the acts of heroism which their victim and his companions had accomplished and which had served to heighten their exasperation, all combined to nerve the hand of the assailants and to add to the diabolical ferocity which characterized his martyrdom.[44]

In 1852, Táhirih, also, was put to death for her blasphemy. Adorned in her wedding dress, she met her persecutors. Handing them the kerchief that symbolized her chastity, Táhirih underlined the meaning of her martyrdom. To her, being strangled by her virginity while wearing her wedding dress *was* her nuptial union with the new creation her actions had helped to release from the misogyny of the old patriarchal tradition.

But when martyrdom is a form of consummation, that consummation has been in the spirit, not in the soul. The trauma released at Badasht was absorbed into a new religion, not into the simple soul-making of men and women.

We strangle ourselves as Táhirih did and identify with the trauma she married through her martyrdom whenever we take apocalyptic emancipation to be a function of faith and virgin purity. The purity of a Táhirih is as vicarious as the meekness that supposedly leads the Christian to spiritual victory.

The movement into soul is not a fulfillment of old laws, not a new dispensation as a final end-point. The soul is never finally unveiled; it is forever a still unravished bride. Soul is a process, not a product, a pregnant virgin, an immaculate whore. Ambivalence and discontinuity, not faith and purity, are the nuptials of the soul. As Blake put it:

> In a wife I would desire
> What in whores is always found—
> The lineaments of gratified desire.[45]

2
Healing through Heresy

The Infectious Savior

After her suicide attempt, shortly before her release from the psychiatric hospital, she dreamed that she sat in a bathtub with light shining out of her nostrils. She found that she was able to take the batteries out of her head, disconnecting the light. The scene changed. Back in her apartment, sitting at the typewriter, she watched workmen replace the glass window panes with white writing paper.

She told her friend the dream. He thought the dream psychotic. He thought that her ability to say the right things to the doctors to gain discharge reflected less her sanity than her deftness at taking batteries out of her flashlight head. He told her that he believed the dream was suggesting that writing could provide a container for what her life could not contain.

Later that evening while reading Northrop Frye's book *The Great Code: The Bible and Literature,* he came upon a passage that brought the dream she had told him back to mind. Writing about Leviathan, the great chaos monster of the oceans, Frye quotes a description of the creature from Job 41 : 18, "... by his sneezings a light doth shine, and his eyelids are like the eyelids of the morning." Setting down the book, he pondered the connection between Leviathan and his friend's dream. "She *is* Leviathan," he thought. "Her psychosis is her identification with him. But how? How is it that this modern woman in a bathtub with batteries in her head manifests the chaos monster?"

He retired to bed, still preoccupied with this question. While sleeping he dreamed. He was on the front lawn of his parents' home. Before him on the grass lay a bathtub, which was completely covered with crosses, Christian crosses. These were drawn on the bathtub so densely that they formed together a cross-hatch or grid design. "Like graph-paper," he thought. Then he had a telephone in his hand. A man from England was on the line. The man said, "The anti-incarnational ideas you are now conceiving are very, very evil." The scene changed, amplifying the dream in other images. He was working on a fishing trawler. Huge catches of fish (fish = Christ) were being heaved on board in nets. The mesh of the nets reminded him of the crosses (or was this but an afterthought upon waking and recalling the dream?). Looking down at his legs, he was fascinated to notice that his blue jeans were entirely patterned with a cross-hatch design of densely arranged crosses. Again the scene changed. He watched an artist make a grid of lines on a drawing. The grid of lines broke the picture into small units. The artist could then transpose the drawing to a larger grid or a smaller one, scaling the picture up or scaling it down.

In the morning he awoke full of dreams, his friend's from the day before and his own from the night past. "Jesus," he thought, "it is through you that the spirit enters flesh, that Leviathan enters bathtubs and persons. Your cross scales the non-human, archetypal world down into man. Are you the carrier and source of the contagion from which we suffer?"

Gnosticism

The Gnostic did not deny trauma. He denied that Christ suffered it for us. In the Acts of John, a work of Christian Apocrypha assigned to the fire by the Nicene Council of 787, the gospel writer takes us to a cave in the Mount of Olives shortly after Jesus was nailed to the cross. In the cave John

THE TOADSTOOL BOOKSHOP
COLONY MILL MARKETPLACE, 222 WEST STREET
KEENE, NH 03431.....PHONE: 603-352-8815
VISIT US IN PETERBOROUGH AND MILFORD
SPECIAL ORDERS WELCOME, GIVE US A CALL

5868   F 12/07/90 11:40

16553 1*ANSW TO JOB   6.95   6.95
18861 1*NEW RUSSIANS   24.95 24.95
6399   2*MAN & HIS SYMBO   19.95 39.90

       4 SUB-TOTAL   71.80
         TAX   .00
         TOTAL   71.80
         Mstr Card-120

Don't forget! From now through Christmas
any book in the store over $60.00 is on
SALE for 20% off the cover price!

wept for his crucified Lord. But when a darkness came over the whole earth, Christ appeared to John, filled the cave with light and said,

> John, for the people below in Jerusalem I am being cruci-
> fied and pierced with lances and reeds and given vinegar
> and gall to drink. But to you I am speaking, and listen to
> what I speak.

Having declared himself, the Christic-phantom (it is am-biguous whether he is corporeal or not) revealed to John the mystery of the cross of light:

> . . . he showed me a cross of light firmly fixed, and around
> the cross a great crowd, which had no single form; and in
> the cross was one form and the same likeness. And I saw
> the Lord himself above the cross, having no shape but only
> a kind of voice; yet not that voice which we knew, but one
> that was sweet and gentle and truly the voice of God,
> which said to me, "John, there must be one man to hear
> these things from me; for I need one who is ready to hear.
> This cross of light is sometimes called logos by me for your
> sakes, sometimes mind, sometimes Jesus, sometimes
> Christ, sometimes a door, sometimes a way, sometimes
> bread, sometimes seed, sometimes resurrection, some-
> times Son, sometimes Father, sometimes Spirit, some-
> times life, sometimes truth, sometimes faith, sometimes
> grace; and so it is called for men's sake."[1]

This revelation is not simply a defense—at least not in the narrow sense. This gospel was written between the second and fourth centuries A.D. and is not the literal story of John's ex-perience on the Mount of Olives. If it were, we would be tempted to see it as an example of denial pure and simple: unable to face the death of his Lord, John denies the crucifixion with a wishful, mystical vision. But this gospel is not reducible to John's security operations. It is not simply the denial of Christ's death and suffering. It is a Gnostic-Docetist rejection of vicarious atonement. The denial is not of death and suffering; denied is the theological conception that salvation has the single formulation of Christ crucified on a wooden cross (i.e., corporeally, once and for all, at a specific time and place in history).

One story is not enough in the Gnostic view. Christ, for the Gnostic, has many names and many faces. He appears to each soul in accordance with the capacity of each soul. In another text from the Apocryphal collection, the Acts of Peter, "Peter" witnesses the Transfiguration of Christ on Mount Tabor. The vision was actually a group vision. A whole crowd witnessed the transfiguration, each in his or her own way. *"Talem eum vidi qualem capere potui,"* Peter explains: "I saw him in such a form as I was able to take in."[2]

The intent of Gnosticism is heresy. By means of a new gospel every day, the Gnostic sought to penetrate out of the reified canon of approved gospels and into the process of *gospelizing.* Gnosticism, first and foremost, is a proliferation of books, an archeological find of fifty-two texts at Nag Hammadi, an embarrassment of riches.

In the place of the dogmatic truth of the wooden cross, Gnosticism places the subtle cross, the cross of light, metaphor. Gnosticism is based not in holy writ, but in the holiness of writing itself. It is not the story of Christ that brings salvation; it is the storying-Christ. The incorporeal (non-incarnate) Gnostic-Jesus is metaphor, and metaphor is the uncanonical solution for the Old Testament trauma, the Old Testament God. Gnosticism is healing fiction.

The nailing of Christ to the wooden cross was, in the Gnostic view, the crucifixion of the capacity to make fiction, the nailing of metaphor, literalism. On the Mount of Olives, Christ reveals this to be the true nature of his suffering:

You hear that I suffered, yet I suffered not; and that I suffered not, yet I did suffer; and that I was pierced, yet I was
not wounded; that I was hanged, yet I was not hanged; that
blood flowed from me, yet it did not flow, and, in a word,
that what they say of me, I did not endure, but what they
do not say, those things I did suffer. Now what these are, I
secretly show you. . . . You must know me, then, as the tor-
ment of the logos, the piercing of the logos, the blood of
the logos, the wounding of the logos, the fastening of the
logos.[3]

Gnostic Analysis

The analyst behind the couch is the gnostic on the Mount of
Olives. The patient lying before him is the corporeal Jesus
nailed to the wooden cross. With benign indifference, the
analyst listens as the patient recounts the history of his incarnational life. Dreams and free-associations are analyzed to
discover the complexes in which spirit is trapped. Ideally,
there is no human relationship between them. A human relationship would only further incarnation. But the job of analysis, or at least of a gnostic analysis, is to liberate spirit,
through metaphor, from the contingency of the patient's life.
Should the analyst leave his station behind the couch, or
should the patient be allowed to engage with the analyst on
personal terms, all metaphors would be instantly attenuated
and the spirit would be trapped in intercourse once more. A
gnostically conceived analysis is anti-coital; its aim is to reveal
the primal scene, interrupt the parental coitus, and free the
soul from its Oedipal bondage.

The royal road to regeneration, dis-carnation, and metaphor
is the anti-relationship which psychoanalysis calls transference. The unknown analyst behind the couch is more than

an idealistic father-imago; he is the father of absence, the gate of the *deus absconditus*. The more the patient speaks to him, the more uncertain the patient becomes. Gradually, the analytic discourse dislocates the sense of necessity that was born alongside his incarnational life until suddenly his words are no longer bound to it at all. The couch becomes a subtle couch, a couch of light, a Mount of Olives, a metaphor. Reclining in the repose of metaphor, the patient is released from the prose of his incarnational life. By restating in poetic terms the incidents of his life which the language of prose had preserved as trauma, the patient frees his soul to follow its desires.

Trauma in Transference

Whatever traumatizes us becomes our parent. Whatever we cannot master with our creative will we turn into a super-parent or god who infantilizes us.

In psychotherapy the patient projects parental imagos on the therapist. Like Job invoking God's good side against His bad side, the patient tries to cuddle up to his trauma in the person of the therapist.

Freud's rejection of the seduction theory moved psychoanalysis behind the couch, a short, yet decisively objective, distance from the traumatic repetition compulsion which the patient was always trying to seduce it into as transference. For Freud to buy the patient's stories about abuse—even if those stories were "true"—would have been to allow himself, in the transference, to be turned into an abuser-in-reverse, the good trauma carrier, the good parent.

Today, more and more, psychotherapy seems to be adopting this model of therapy that Freud eschewed. Many therapists today describe what they do as "re-parenting." Therapy as re-parenting can take any number of forms, from the subtle sophistication of object relations theory to the concrete literalism of an Esalen re-birthing weekend. Though there is as much disagreement about how best to re-parent as there is about how it is best to parent, there is agreement about basic principles. The patient must regress to early fixation points and re-experience them in the relationship of basic trust that is established with the therapist.

The problem with this model of therapy is that the patient merely adopts a good parent to replace the bad; nothing is experienced, save the identification defenses implicit to the original trauma. No wonder the so-called transference neurosis is so hard to resolve. More and more therapy hours must be sacrificed to mollify the hunger of the reified trauma—the fierce incest wishes of the transference. Of course, analysis becomes an interminable endeavor.

After an initial honeymoon period, the trauma, which re-parenting would seem to have healed, constellates again as if conspicuous in its absence. The patient, not really having absorbed the trauma at all, starts to test the therapist to make certain he is really the good parent. This testing can take a variety of forms, dependency and/or seduction being particularly common.

Today we do not need to go to the extreme Freud required in order to step out of the parent role. We can remain behind the couch with Freud, objectively detached, without denying the reality of our patient's early trauma and victimizations. In fact, I believe, we can become even colder, less parental, and more therapeutic if we *do* acknowledge it. What, after all, is analytic detachment when all it is detached from is the patient's auto-erotic fantasy? Freud became a parent to his hysterical patients in spite of himself through the patronizing attitude he must certainly have had to adopt to treat women whom he believed to be merely the victims of their own perverse wishes to be seduced. Today, after more than eighty years of psychoanalysis, we can recognize trauma with the early Freud and refuse to become its vicarious antidote with the later Freud. As we hand the transference back to the patient again and again, as we meticulously refuse to be adopted as the white-washed replacement for the trauma that has orphaned her, we create an arena in which the trauma can finally be experienced and assimilated.

It is not that we should treat the trauma by re-parenting the patient; rather, we should treat the trauma by dislocating it from the parent–child tandem in which it tries to repeat itself, but in which it is too infantilized, on the one hand, and too reified, on the other, to be experienced.

The main work of psychotherapy is de-literalizing the parent problem, de-literalizing the tendency of the patient to form covenantal relationships with the events that he has as yet been unable to experience.

Jeffrey Moussaieff Masson

When we read Masson's book *The Assault on Truth: Freud's Suppression of the Seduction Theory,* we are taken down into Jerusalem to the scene of a crucifixion. Freud's letters to Fliess recounting the complications suffered by Emma Eckstein due to their treatment of her are nothing less than horrific. Equally appalling is the material in the chapter which reviews the early literature of child abuse. Reading Masson's account of the origins of psychoanalysis, we are overwhelmed by the trauma—both in the etiology of the cases and, in the instance of Emma Eckstein, in the treatment.

How is it that Freud could recant his seduction theory when it was so clearly grounded in the empirical record? Was it simply out of a failure of courage and a loyalty to Fliess as Masson argues?

Psychoanalysts generally view Freud's rejection of the seduction theory and his discovery of the pathogenic power of fantasy as the foundation of psychoanalysis. The move from seduction in the outer sense of sexual abuse at the hands of others to seduction in the inner sense of disturbances caused by one's own drive fantasies was the beginning of what we call modern psychology.

Like the gospel writer of the Acts of John, Freud's thought moved from the wooden cross of Jerusalem to the subtle cross of the Mount of Olives; that is, Freud moved from the carnal intelligence of the traumatic happenings that neither he nor his patients were able to absorb to a subtle, metaphorical intelligence, an intelligence that was able to absorb the literal traumatic events by transmuting them into fantasies.

Freud's rejection of the seduction theory stemmed from the fact that he did not adequately distinguish between events and experiences. He evaluated the authenticity of the traumatic events his patients remembered in analysis as if these events were *experiences*. Since the events, considered from the inside (i.e., psychoanalytically), did not meet the outer criterion of being an experience, Freud came to doubt the reality of the events themselves. As he wrote to Fliess, "there are no indications of reality in the unconscious, so that one cannot distinguish between truth and fiction that has been cathected with affect."[4] Freud came to deny the material reality of the traumas his patients reported because at that time he did not yet have a sufficient concept of psychological reality to bridge the difference between the external events and the fantasies about them which were making them into soul. In hindsight we can see Freud's rejection of the material basis of his patient's memories as the extremity necessary at the time (but no longer necessary today) to break out of his nineteenth-century materialism and into the reality of the psyche where events are made into experiences.

A trauma, by definition, is overwhelming and for the most part outside the available parameters of experience. Repression, it follows, is less a defensive procedure than an awkward terminology for expressing that an event lacks the sufficient field of comparison (i.e., the sufficient phenomenology) to be experienced as a phenomenon. A traumatic event is not pushed out of awareness; rather, it is too big to register in awareness. Traumata only return from repression when a sufficient inventory of comparable events provides a reality schema that can more or less absorb them. The so-called repetition compulsion is a way of trying to create a field of comparable events in whose terms the traumatic event can be relativized and experienced. Of course, in the transference sexually abused patients manufacture fictitious seduction scenes and attempt to seduce their therapists. They act out what they cannot remember because it was too overwhelming to be properly experienced. They are trying to heal themselves.

Simply exposing the heinous deeds of seduction is of little help therapeutically. Therapy's concern is with absorbing the events, experiencing them. To play the good parent and point out to the patient in love and compassion that he has suffered an intolerable trauma is to confine his experience and the integration of his trauma to a good-parent/bad-parent split in conformity with society's disgust and horror. This kind of therapeutic maneuver merely shifts the trauma from matter to spirit. The patient identifies with his good parent or savior therapist and hovers now as far above the trauma as he once stooped over beneath it. 'Born again,' a crusader for the oppressed or for this or that moralistic fanaticism, the patient has merely identified with the whitewashed and reified version of what he could not absorb. Therapy has become vicarious religion, and inasmuch as the patient has forfeited to it the drive to experience the events he has suffered (i.e., his repetition compulsion), he has lost his soul.

Today, as heirs to the Freudian psychological legacy, we can help our abused patients transmute their traumas into experiences. We can affirm the reality of child sexual assault and the mental disturbances that may accompany it precisely because we have been eighty years on the Mount of Olives with Freud.

Freud's disavowal of the seduction theory was not an "assault on truth" as Jeffrey Masson argues. It was the discovery of the metaphorical basis of the mind necessary to ground life's material (and spiritual) traumas in a fashion that heals them. The psychoanalytic maxim that the patient is always lying is a Docetist move that takes the patient out of his historicized, and therefore myopic, reading of a traumatic event into the fictional mode called "interpretation" which turns the event into an experience.

"You hear that I suffered, yet I suffered not; and that I suffered not, yet I did suffer...." Psychoanalysis eschews the crucifixion of the logos, the subordination of metaphorical language to the forensic reportage of "what happened." Psychoanalysis is a "talking cure," a re-writing of paralyzing events into experiences that let life go on.

Abandoning Seduction

There are dreams, I believe, which beg the rejection of the so-called seduction theory. A child can appear hungry, hurt, abused or abandoned.[5] Like Freud affirming the seduction theory a final time before rejecting it, we too say with Goethe, "What have they done to you, poor child?"[6]

Like Freud, we at first take the suffering child too literally. Hunger and hungering, hurt and hurting, abuse and abusing, abandonment and abandoning—these, as they are carried by the child, are *events,* even literal events, but not *experiences.* In childhood our first 'experience' is our last and, therefore, not really an experience at all.

Just as Freud looked for trauma in early childhood—only then to claim that the traumas were for the most part invented fantasies and screen memories—we can regard the afflicted child of our dreams and fantasies as the carrier of the events of our lives (whether material or spiritual) that we have not yet experienced. What has happened to us that is still young and inexperienced and that if we attempt to rescue or help remains immature and unexperienced?

The child brings back to us the childish things that now as adults we can put aside, experience, absorb. So long as we try to save or feed the child, we facilitate the repetition of the events associated with the child. We get more and more needy.

The parent is the vicarious religion of the child. What the child can't handle the parent will handle for it. The two figures construct each other. The parent is a sort of child-in-reverse, shielding the child from experience, bringing it up to be afraid of the same things that the parent, now regressed and identified with its child, is afraid of.

Unabsorbable events (the abandoned child exposed to the elements) do not necessarily have to be the result of forensically defined neglect or victimization. The unbearable want of the dream child can be like the "unbearable lightness of being" in Milan Kundera's novel by the same title. When a child-like lover floats into the protagonist Tomas's life, "like a child someone had put in a bulrush basket daubed with pitch and sent downstream for [him] to fetch at the riverbank of his bed," the narrator comments: "We can never know what to want, because, living only one life, we can neither compare it with our previous lives nor perfect it in our lives to come."[7] The experiencing of events is always a function of the availability of comparable events, and hence a fiction.

Abandoning the needy child, even as Freud abandoned the seduction theory, is a move that takes us into soul. "Yes, it happened, but is the historical punctuation the only punctuation? Does the event admit another reading? Will it become more absorbable when we break it down with a number of interpretations?"

Kissing our traumas better is a vicarious trick of grace which robs them of their possibilities for soul. Going with events homoerotically, however, turns them into experiences. Like cures like because like *experiences* like.

Eucharist and Globus Hystericus

At the age of twelve he experienced a severe trauma. A piece of food became lodged over his windpipe, choking him. The episode lasted a dangerously long time. Finally, however, the boy's mother was able to dislodge the obstruction so that he could breathe again. From behind his newspaper, the boy's father, stern with fear, had been yelling at his wife not to hit their son so hard on the back. After catching his breath, the boy yelled back at his father: "What would you have her do— not save my life?"

From that day on the boy had difficulty swallowing, particularly when he ate with his father. From the family systems point of view of Murry Bowen, this boy was the "projected child," the child designated by the family to absorb its emotional fusion, the child through whom the marital conflict was short-circuiting. From the psychoanalytic point of view, trauma at the phallic stage of development (perhaps adding itself to earlier conflicts returning from repression with the reconstellation of the Oedipus-complex at puberty) interrupted the normal resolution of the Oedipus-complex. While normally a son would have aligned himself with his father by this time in order not to have him as an adversary, this boy perceived his father as too threatening for identification to occur. From yet a third point of view, the point of view of vicarious religion, Christ had died on the cross that this boy might have life more abundant. If he could only take Jesus into his life, Jesus would heal him by suffering it for him.

The boy was interested in this third possibility. He had been raised in the church; he knew the Christian story. At some level he even felt close to Jesus. Both were, after all, passover lambs—Jesus taking on the sins and sufferings of the world, the choking boy the emotional fusion of his family system. Surely Christianity could resolve the boy's Oedipus-complex. Christ also had a murdering father and yet was able to commend his spirit into his father's hands while being crucified by His design. Vicarious religion, however, did not heal the boy —though not for a lack of prayer and supplication, both personal and intercessory.

When he was sixteen he had a dream. In the dream he was back at the friend's house he had been in the evening before. They were having the same conversation about world religions. The evening before the dream, the friend (a recent convert to transcendental meditation) had explained that there are three million gods in the Hindu pantheon, though all can be considered aspects of the one deity, Brahman. In the dream the party of friends decide to move their conversation from the kitchen/family room into the living room so as not to disturb the young host's parents who were sleeping in a room nearby. As he was walking out of the room and into the hallway leading to the living room, the dreamer noticed an arching doorway and beyond that a small stone chapel. At the front of the little chapel a cross was erected in the chancel. The peculiar thing about the cross was that it was dismantled; the crosspiece to which the hands of Christ were supposedly nailed was lying down on the floor. The cross was beautiful, and it emitted a holy light that illuminated the whole room.

Of course, the dreamer did not understand the dream intellectually. He had never heard of the Gnostics, let alone of the Docetist theology of the cross of light. Yet he did experience their revelation. The Hindu idea that God has three million faces must have triggered the dream. The idea is comparable to the notion presented in the Acts of Peter that each soul perceives God (Jesus) in such a form as it is able to take in. After this dream the boy's relation to his symptom lost its orthodoxy and changed. The cross, having been dismantled, could no longer serve as a model for his suffering or as a model for his vicarious salvation from suffering. If there were at least three million stories through which to experience God (i.e., the trauma he had learned to call God), what was his particular story?

While down in Jerusalem Christ was being nailed to a wooden cross and a twelve-year-old boy was gagging on his Oedipus-complex, up on the Mount of Olives the same boy (though now sixteen) was realizing in a dream that the secret nature of his suffering was the crucifixion of the imagination by a single, reified, authorized version of the soul's atonement, the literalization of the logos.

The boy had literary ambitions. He wanted to be a writer. But how had the writing been going on for the past four years? It had been going on elaborately in a thousand little avoidance behaviors a day. The calligraphy in which he wrote his life had been a subversive calligraphy of hiding his symptoms and propitiating his trauma. For years he had lived a very circumscribed life, avoiding social engagements that would involve food. He had become the scribe of his trauma, utterly subservient to the dictates of the creative power he had renounced and projected into the unpalatable eucharist of vicarious religion.

The capacity within himself to absorb his own trauma, the capacity within himself to create his own sustaining fiction, had been rendered outcast, subversive, illegitimate and ineffectual by the story of Christ crucified. What he had been unable to swallow was the eucharist of vicarious theology.

After the dream of the dismantled cross, the boy's attention turned away from his symptom somewhat. More and more energy began to flow into writing. He wrote a black-humored novel about his symptom, comparable in some respects to Kafka's *Metamorphosis*. Sentence by sentence he transfigured into art the creative energy that had been incarnated into a neurotic lifestyle. Finally, enough writing had been done to render the body of his affliction into the simulacrum of a body. His symptoms had become a fiction. The *globus hystericus* had been cured by the wafer of soul-making, metaphor.

Do-It-Yourself

In the dream he carefully drew a serpentine line on a piece of paper, a line that snaked back and forth like a serpent. A friend looked at the line with him, and together they adjusted it, making it even more serpentine. The scene changed. The dreamer found himself in a small-town Protestant church. The sanctuary was bright and lovely and full of the activity of a lively, singing congregation. The sanctuary itself was very plain. He didn't recall any stained glass or religious objects. Although the congregation was entirely Caucasian, they reminded him of a congregation of black gospel singers, so soulful was their music. He was enjoying the service immensely.

A cousin of his, a woman whom he had not seen since he was a child, sang a beautiful solo. Although she was the dreamer's cousin, her appearance was quite different. She had marked Jewish features (the dreamer was from a thoroughly Christian background) and was obviously mentally retarded. This mental deficiency did not detract at all from her singing; in fact, her moronic face smiled as if it were completely congruent with the pleasure of her song. Then the dreamer walked up to the table in the chancel. Although the communion table is the place of Christianity's central sacrament, this one was very plain. As communion tables go, it too was a smiling moron. On the table was a muffin, homemade, wholesome, and decorated with variously colored icing. He picked it up and tasted it. The pleasant taste of the muffin was consistent with the pleasure and gaiety of the whole service—the warmth of community, the beauty of his cousin's voice and face, the songs themselves.

There are, of course, many ways to read this dream. One obvious way would be to see it as a demonic parody of Christianity—to see the snake as evil, the muffin as blasphemed eucharist, the dream itself as the sin against the Holy Ghost. Such an interpretation, however, is grounded in an orthodoxy that is foreign to the dream. Rather than measuring the dream's images against the reified sacramental standards they seem to be standing in for, let us stay closer to the images as they are, unconverted, un-amplified. This is not to deny that in this specific dream the conventional theological and sacramental forms are very present in their absence. The religious forms which the dream's images seem to be standing in for are indeed precisions of the dream's actual images. An essential aspect of the dream-church is that it lacks the sanctimonious quality we usually associate with a church. Everything about the dream-church is mundane; nothing is numinous. The architectural structure of the building expresses no heavenly striving. No heavenly scenes ornament the windows in stained glass. No cross is displayed as a focus of worship. *Nothing whatsoever in this church is vicarious.* The eucharist is a homemade muffin; the music is homespun soul; the service is an informal service without a presiding clergyperson. Even the soloist is a relative, a cousin of the dreamer.

In this do-it-yourself church, there is no sense of displaced, reified suffering and vicarious atonement. The reach of the spirit has not exceeded the grasp of soul-making. A conjectured God does not reach beyond the parishioners' creating wills. There is no excess of God to be killed by some Nietzschean madman.

In his poem "Esthetique du mal," Wallace Stevens takes up the same theme as does this dream. In explanation of his observation that "heaven and hell / Are one, and here, O terra infidel," Stevens writes:

> The fault lies with an over-human god
> Who by sympathy has made himself a man
> And is not to be distinguished, when we cry
>
> Because we suffer, our oldest parent, peer

Of the populace of the heart, the reddest lord,
Who has gone before us in experience.

If only he would not pity us so much,
Weaken our fate, relieve us of woe both great
And small, a constant fellow of destiny,

A too, too human god, self-pity's kin
And uncourageous genesis. . . .
It seems As if the health of the world might be enough.

It seems as if the honey of common summer
Might be enough, as if the golden combs
Were part of a sustenance itself enough,

As if hell, so modified, had disappeared,
As if pain, no longer satanic mimicry,
Could be borne, as if we were sure to find our way.[8]

If it were not for the "too human god" of vicarious theology,
the "honey of common summer"—the pleasures of the imagination, the muffin, and the song—would be enough to
carve out a human habitation within the traumatic level of existence. In the dream and in Stevens's poem, vicarious religion
is rejected in favor of the pleasure principle—soul-making,
aesthetics, poetry, art. This is the serpent's wisdom, the
serpentine, Gnostic line. Trauma, in the view of Gnostic-
Docetism, cannot be packed off once and for all onto the
shoulders of Christ crucified. Nor can a limited canon of approved gospels absorb "chance, and death, and mutability."
The meaning of a gospel is another gospel. Trauma involves us
in an endless, serpentine process, and the creative efforts of
the imagination reflect the interminable dialectic between the
reality and pleasure principles.

The imagination is like the song of our moronic, Jewish
cousin. Her blank mind is the erasure of the Old Testament

history of covenants with the displaced trauma we have learned to call God. Had Moses heard this cousin's singing, he might never have needed to bring the tablets down from Sinai. Had the Children of Israel heard this cousin's singing, they might never have needed to worship the calf they made. For, from the perspective of her song, both engagements are vicarious conjecturings, conceits of belief rather than creations of the imagination for the soul's delight.

Romanticism

He went to a lecture at the university on the poetry of the English Romantics. The lecturer suggested that the theme of Romanticism, whatever its content, was the process of its own making. The poets, he said, were writing about writing. They were trying to build a temple for the soul "Where branched thoughts, new grown with pleasant pain,/Instead of pines shall murmur in the wind." The lecturer quoted a passage from John Keats's famous letter:

> Call the world if you Please "The vale of Soul-making" Then you will find out the use of the world (I am speaking now in the highest terms for human nature admitting it to be immortal which I will here take for granted for the purpose of showing a thought which has struck me concerning it) I say "*Soul-making*" Soul as distinguished from an Intelligence—There may be intelligences or sparks of divinity in millions—but they are not Souls till they acquire identities, till each one is personally itself. I[n]telligences are atoms of perception—they know and they see and they are pure, in short, they are God—How then are Souls to be made? How then are these sparks which are God to have identity given them—so as ever to possess a bliss peculiar to each one's individual existence?

How, but by the medium of a world like this? This point I
sincerely wish to consider because I think it a grander
system of salvation than the chrysteain religion....[9]

Later that night, at home in bed, he drifted off into the
culture, he drifted off into a dream. On the lawn beside St.
Paul's Anglican Church, a tent was pitched and tightly zip-
pered up. In the grass around the tent lay money—loose coins,
change. He was with friends. He and they were local boys.
They were maverick, delinquent and uproarious. The scene
changed. He was listening to the repetition of last evening's
lecture on the Romantics. While the lecturer spoke, he held
the dreamer's head tightly between his hands. This show of af-
fection was slightly embarrassing to the dream-ego. At last, the
lecturer released his hold and the dreamer swooned. The
hands had been holding the dreamer's head very tightly, cutting off the blood. The dreamer struggled to remain conscious
and did manage to keep his wits. Then he noticed an article
written by the lecturer titled "Elegy." With the article was a
polemic by a literary critic condemning the piece as mad or
evil. Female custodians, fascinated with the lecture, allowed
the talk to go on past the university's usual closing time. Finally, the lecture ended and the lecturer invited a dark woman
to join him and they left together.

Then the time orientation shifted back to the middle of the
lecture. The dreamer left the lecture hall, perhaps to use a
washroom, perhaps because he was still dizzy from the lecturer's hold on his head. He entered a very small room or cell.
The walls were old and covered with graffiti. A single, naked
light-bulb hung down as a source of light. Reaching down into
his trousers he examined his scrotum. He felt his testicles and
found with them in his scrotum a third one and a fourth. Then
a voice said flatly and with objective intonation: "The God of
the Christian religion is no god at all." Over and over again the
voice repeated the statement: "The God of the Christian relig-

ion is no god at all." He thought it important to remember the statement.

Beside him on the floor there was some cheap newsprint-quality paper. With a pen he started to write down the sentence—"The God of the Christian religion"—but before he could record the whole sentence the earliest words began to vanish. The paper wouldn't take the ink. Again he tried to write the sentence down. Again and again, repetitively, compulsively. But the ink would not take. He noticed, however, that as he wrote the paper became of finer and finer quality until at last it attained a satin finish. Worried that he was going mad and that he would not be able to find his way out of the little closet (or even record the sentence that might hold the key to releasing him), he awoke with a fright.

After hearing a lecture on the Romantics, after hearing how Wordsworth tapped the hiding places of power for the refreshment of his soul's life, the dreamer finds himself in the yard outside St. Paul's Anglican Church even as Coleridge, in his Mariner's Rime, let himself slip "below the Kirk, below the hill, below the lighthouse top" to the wellsprings of the creative imagination. When the dreamer resides outside the Church among his Gnostic brethren in the "vale of Soul-making," there is money in the grass, loose change. In the "vale of Soul-making," in that place of a salvation grander than that of the "chrystean religion," change is loosed and value freed from the sacramental containers of the Church.

Inside the lecture hall, the contents of the dreamer's head push out even as the lecturer's hands squeeze in around it and tighten the focus. The pressure in the dreamer's head builds up, like the multiplication of the loose change in the grass, and makes him dizzy. He swoons and nearly passes out. The Romantic vision of the possibilities of soul-making is releasing his soul from its Christian parameters. An article titled "Elegy" catches the dreamer's attention. The lecturer is reciting an elegy, releasing the imagination by announcing the death of its old containers: the Christian Church and the Christian God.

The soul's release is the feminine's return. The female custodians step out of their janitorial roles, enter the Academy, and listen to the talk. Their release from patriarchal domination is what soul-making is all about. A fundamental taboo of totemism has been removed. The lecturer and the dark woman go off together as equals.

In the middle of the whole process, the dreamer leaves the lecture hall and, in a small cell or closet covered with the genital grammar (graffiti) of patriarchy, takes down his trousers and examines his testicles. There are four of them. Unlike Abraham's servant who placed his hand under Abraham's thigh to swear a solemn oath upon the patriarch's testicles, the dreamer places his hand under his own thigh. The whole covenantal tradition, the whole tradition of projecting and reifying creativity, is dislocating into his scrotum. Money in the grass, pressure in the head, a doubling of the testicles: each image is a commentary on the others. No longer are there testicles above him. The testicles of God, like the tablets of Moses, have smashed to pieces like loose change in the grass. The soul has been released from the reified, codified, authorized traditions of the spirit into the multiple and individual possibilities of the imagination and soul-making. Like Aphrodite-Venus emerging from the severed testicles of the sky-father Uranus, the female custodians and the dark woman emerge also. Charwomen are now sages.

"The God of the Christian religion is no god at all." The sentence is a declaration of freedom, freedom from the genital grammar of monotheistic tyranny. Any God who takes the imagination captive is not a god at all.

He tries to write the sentence down but he cannot. The ink will not take. Again he tries and again. He worries that he is going mad. Without God, without boundaries and limiting structures, there is uncertainty. Anything is possible. Perhaps, he thinks, simply writing down the declaration that the God is no god will give him a point of certainty, a standpoint. But soul-making will not be reified into truth-statements.The new wine will not be placed in the old bottles. With every sentence that will not take to the page, the dreamer is further abandoned to the process of writing and the uncertainties of the imagination (the question: what does the soul want?). Again and again he tries to write down a positive declaration, and each time the sentence vanishes. Over time, however, the paper transforms, becoming of finer and finer quality. The dreamer's soul, by long apprenticeship to uncertainty, coagulates into the substantiality and quality of satin-finish paper. It is precisely this process of interminable writing or soul-making that is the dreamer's way of stepping over the threshold of the reified trauma and out of the Great Code.

The Pleasure of Dis-carnation

In the body, where Freud located the pleasure principle, pleasure means instinctual satisfaction—drive reduction. In the spirit, where vicarious theology locates the pleasure principle, pleasure means belief in supernatural consolations and the futurity of illusion. It is not necessary, however, to define pleasure solely in terms of the body or the spirit. Pleasure need not be restricted to the discharge of instinctual dynamisms, an orgasm to end all orgasms, an apocalyptic rapture, or a gospel to end all gospels. Experienced within the perspective of the realm between body and spirit, the realm of soul or metaphor, pleasure is simply an aesthetic response, a breathing in,[10] a saving of the phenomena (rather than a reifying into physical or spiritual categories), a process with no end point.

In *The Ego and the Id,* Freud discusses how when "satisfaction triumphs . . . Eros is eliminated, and the death instinct has a free hand for accomplishing its purposes."[11] Freud illustrates his point by referring to the fact that the praying mantis and the drone bee die immediately after copulation. The literalization of instinct and pleasure into an energy model answerable to the law of entropy culminates finally in the reduction of all tension, "nirvana," and death. As Rollo May notes at this point in his reflections (*Beyond the Pleasure Principle*), Freud introduced the concept of Eros, a life-force which opposes the death-drive by introducing "fresh tensions."[12]

Like the Gnostic writer to whom the Docetist vision of Christ's transfiguration was revealed, Freud's vision of Eros was a Docetist transfiguration of his earlier, physiologically literalized (incarnational) conception of the Id and the pleasure principle. While down in the Jerusalem of a merely carnal intelligence a praying mantis and a drone bee were being crucified by the climax of corporeal satisfaction, up in a cave on the Mount of Olives, Eros, the pleasure principle in its subtle, metaphorical sense, was being revealed to Freud.

Baptism

Freudian analysis—the recollection of childhood memories —is an attempt to turn early events into experiences. In analysis the patient is born into the *experience* of his life. This 'second birth,' however, is not to be confused with the religious sense of re-birth. Religious re-birth is a flight from the experience of one's own existence into spirit. In the sacrament of baptism, the soul is immunized against the "evils" and vicissitudes of the material world. Before our first life has properly begun, a second birth is imposed. As soon as possible, we must be insulated by our spiritual birth from the perils of our animal birth. Stated positively, the soul is naturally Christian (Tertullian). Stated negatively, unbaptized babies do not have souls, cannot be redeemed, and dwell in limbo after death.

The aim of analysis is to recall memories from the repression of baptism. Analysis is anti-baptismal. The patient is not christened in terms of the Father, the Son, and the Holy Ghost; he is differentiated from them. Only when the Father, Son, and Holy Ghost are divested of their numinosity are we born into experience, born into soul.

To be born into the soul is very different from being born into matter or spirit. The soul is a process, not a product. It is a pregnant virgin, a "mystic writing pad upon" which events register themselves as experiences and, then, partially erase themselves so that more experiences are possible. Nothing is hewn in stone or written into tablets.

While the birth into spirit may be as ecstatic as the birth into matter was traumatic, the birth into soul is more dis-passionate. We may feel cold, dis-carnate, suspended between two worlds (matter and spirit), stuck in the birth canal.

For Freud the goal of analysis was to return the patient to "normal unhappiness." Analysis does not baptize the soul, nor does it redeem or "save" it. Analysis takes the patient into events for the sake of experience, into the soul for its own sake. It assigns us to the limbo of our own creative will.

Normal Unhappiness

Because therapy's traumatic content tends to take on a religious formulation and to demand cure in the most vicar-ious forms possible, psychotherapy is often seduced into considering itself a road to salvation. The human potential movement especially has contributed to the spiritualizing of psychotherapy. The agendas and goals of today's therapies are an embarrassment of riches: peak experiences, androgyny, in-dividuation, wholeness, self-realization, nirvana, intimacy, transparency, love, assertiveness, mysticism, mind/body unity, left brain/right brain coherence, self-actualization, growth, happiness, etc. The problem with ideal goals is that they may be nothing more than inflated avoidances of the very difficulties which have occasioned interest in them in the first place. Why all this fervor, numinosity, and missionary zeal? What is all this religious kitsch attempting to cover?

Rather than meeting the patient's desire for atonement, rather than helping the patient to become 'reborn' into a reaction formation against the very disturbance he cannot absorb, therapy must pull the rug out from under the patient's vicarious eurekas and frustrate his flight to atonement, the so-called flight into health.

A caring pessimism in the therapist can bring to therapy a sobering counterweight to the patient's tendency to project, reify, and identify with whitewashed versions of his difficulties. That attitude of "cool benevolence" and "benign indifference"—so characteristic of Freud—can, like the voice of Daedalus, help restrain the flights of those patients who, like Icaros, would fly too near the reified versions of the very symptoms they believe they are recovering from.

To many, the goal of returning patients to "normal unhappiness" will seem too modest. After all, there is more to life than "normal unhappiness." It is my belief, however, that this "more" should be left to the patient to find or, rather, to make. The work of therapy, even a Jungian-oriented therapy, should be mainly *reductive*. We must confront the tendency of the patient's spiritual flights to exceed the reach of his soul-making.

To be returned to normal unhappiness means to be returned to the creative burden of one's own existence. No longer is 'health' or 'illness' attributed to causes that lie beyond the tactics of one's own creative responses. Normal unhappiness is a state in which the positive and negative inflations of the vicarious life have been transformed into the poles of the coordinating pleasure principle of one's own creative life.

It is not in the patient's life that we wish him happiness —that would be too vicarious. The goal of "normal unhappiness" shifts the very location of happiness away from the simple givenness of life to the process of life's making, the process of soul-making, what Freud called *"die sache"* ("the work") and what Jung called the "opus," more important than any goal.

Dreams

What is the 'right' dream interpretation? When the patient is held in thrall by the trauma-God, the 'right' interpretation is the one that kills God and releases the creative power displaced on Him back into human hands, back into the hands of the dreamer. Too often dream interpretation degenerates into vicarious religion. Many Jungians, for instance, consider dreams to be messages from what they call the empirical god-image, the archetype of the Self. According to the Jungian point of view, dreams tell us what to do or, at least, how to adjust our one-sided ego-attitudes. Freudians, on the other hand, believe that the purpose of dreams is to protect sleep from the vicissitudes of the instincts by sating them with images. Freudian analysis looks to the dream to provide messages about the development of the libido. When the "dreamwork" is untangled by the work of interpretation, the patient is confronted with his infantile fixations and encouraged to sublimate them into maturer forms of expression.

Both the Jungian and the Freudian perspectives anchor dreams in meta-psychological models of psychic structure that are taken literally. But meta-psychologies are *conjectures* which posit the psyche and the dream beyond the reach of man's creating will. Models of the psyche and theories of personality are attempts to form a conceptual (conjectural) relationship to the creative power we have projected beyond ourselves. Psychological theories are projections superimposed upon an even more fundamental projection—the disowned capacity of the creative imagination to create reality. I am not merely saying that the map is not the territory. I am saying there is no territory. It is we who are the 'divine' artificers, we who are the makers of what is humanly real (notwithstanding that our characters can get away on us!).

Dreams immerse us in the chaos necessary to the work of re-creation. Dreams are crazy. They break all the rules of the objective world, the world perceived by Coleridge's reifying primary imagination as the "repetition in the finite mind of the eternal act of creation in the infinite I AM."[13] Every night the "day residues" (Freud), the images borrowed from the day before, return to us in distortion. The covenant between the signifiers and the objects they supposedly signify breaks down. Even the crucifix dislocates itself into an image of the crucifix or, better, into an image *as* crucifix.[14] Everything is rendered subject to the creating will. Interpretation is literally everything.

"I fear," wrote Nietzsche, "that we are not getting rid of God because we still believe in grammar." The grammar of dream interpretation, whether Freudian or Jungian, is a crust of dead theology. We deaden the outer surfaces of our creative response to dreams in order to protect ourselves from the creative power the dreams bring back to us.

Nietzsche feared the coming of a time "when man will no longer launch the arrow of his longing beyond man—and the string of his bow will have unlearned how to whizz."[15] Every dream is a quiver of arrows, a quiver of wishes, a quiver of longings. Dream interpretation should put the whizz back into our bowstrings. It is the job of interpretation to arrow images beyond man's operative consciousness. The 'right' interpretation is the most daring interpretation. A new dream interpretation should be like a new precedent in the law: Mr. Smith versus the State of California; Mr. Jones versus Freud and Jung. Therapists are lawyers who help emancipate the dream from the prison of status quo interpretations. Dream interpretation is the space project of an ever-opening consciousness. Interpretations are trajectories, arrows of longing, satellites in

the surrendered heaven of man's creating will. Dream interpretation is metaphor-making.

Nuclear Escalation

Nuclear arms, world-destroying power in the hands of man,
can be viewed as a transitional stage between vicarious
religion and soul-making. With nuclear weapons man swal-
lows God; man becomes his own God, his own danger, his own
trauma. With nuclear arms man releases himself from the
vicarious supports of religion. No longer can he conceive of
himself in a covenantal relationship with an omnipotent God.
No longer can he look away from his own power and responsibility to the power and responsibility he projects into God.
Grace has become extinct in this century.

At a certain point in the cold war between the United States
and the Soviet Union, at a certain point in the stockpiling of
nuclear weapons, the magnitude of God was transcended. Today our creative power, our destructive power, exceeds the
power we have displaced on God. No longer does the God of
man's conjecturing reach beyond the power of man's own
creating will.

God *was* big, even as the First and Second World Wars were
big. It took the systematic extermination of millions of Jews,
Poles, Japanese, homosexuals and Gypsies—not to mention
the soldiers who died in action—for mankind to feel anything.
Only when our human tragedy had become slightly larger
than the capacity of our religious containers to absorb it were
we able to *experience* our humanity. Ironically, with the
death camps and the bomb, man gave himself back to himself.

The twentieth-century stockpile of nuclear arms is bigger
than God. Today we can feel the burden of our creative/
destructive power. Individuating a relationship to our immense power involves the global community in a tremendous

world of soul-making. A renaissance is enacting itself today in terms of the escalation and de-escalation of the arms race.

In 1944, Jung could still write that, "Despite appearances to the contrary, the establishment of order and the dissolution of what has been established are at bottom beyond human control." If today we can no longer share Jung's conviction on this point it is because, as Jung writes in his next sentence, we are now aware that "... only that which can destroy itself is truly alive."[16]

Meaning

The search for meaning—what a vicarious notion! Is it here? Is it there, lying about waiting to be discovered? The pearl of great price and the treasure hard to attain are delusions (traumatic ideas of reference) at the end of a rainbow which keep us locked into a quest for things which don't exist, but must be invented. Reality is our own creation. That is the bitterest pill—the toughest eucharist—to swallow, but it is also the most medicinal and transubstantiating.

Deliver Us from Salvation

It was once believed by many that the rewards of the spirit come from good works. But the idea that heaven could be purchased by good behavior contained an even more fundamental idea—the idea that God could be paid off with protection money. Religion degenerated into a kind of insurance policy. Priests, like indemnity underwriters of a mafia godfather, sold sow's ear indulgences to their parishioners who wanted to sin without compromising their places in heaven. Luther, appalled by this salvation-mongering, argued that we are justified not by good works or sow's ears, but by faith. God, for Luther, could not be bought or sold, nor could salvation. Fear of God, alone, he held to be the prerequisite for salvation, and faith was entirely God's gift.

The notion of salvation is eternally corruptible. The priest can wholesale it, and Calvin can go to the opposite extreme and argue that it is doled out by the whim of a stingy God to an elect few. Indeed, each denomination has fostered allegiance in itself through its teachings about salvation. But how many theological hairs will have to be split before we realize that what we need salvation from is the very notion of salvation itself? Soul-making burns the salvific bridge that theology would erect between the sacred and the profane, this world and the next. In soul-making we are justified neither by good works nor by spiritual election, but, rather, by fiction. "The images that yet/fresh images beget" is the only salvation soul-making offers. How we dramatize ourselves to ourselves, how the soul imagines our lives, how we dream events into experiences—that is what justifies the anti-salvation that is soul-making. Grounding in fiction, in life as fiction, saves us from the fantasy of truth and from the fantasy (which forgets it is a fantasy) of a saving truth. We make soul by releasing it from the pretensions of a salvation that would save it.

3
Repeating, Imagining, and Making a Crust

The Crust around the Pleasure Principle

The phenomenon of repetition compulsion led Freud to posit a death-instinct. In the repetition of traumatic events and destructive behaviors, Freud saw the organism striving to return to a state of inorganic matter.

> But how is the predicate of being "instinctual" related to the compulsion to repeat? At this point we cannot escape a suspicion that we may have come upon the track of a universal attribute of instincts and perhaps of organic life in general.... *It seems, then, that an instinct is an urge inherent in organic life to restore an earlier state of things* which the living entity has been obliged to abandon under the pressure of external disturbing forces; that is, it is a kind of organic elasticity, or, to put it in another way, the expression of the inertia inherent in organic life.[1]

Originally, instincts were very close to inorganic matter, so close, in fact, that Freud defined them as the tendency to return to inorganic matter. The fact that complex life forms have developed despite this inertia Freud attributes to "the pressure of external disturbing forces" which makes the path to death and the inorganic state of things more and more circuitous:

> The attributes of life were at some time evoked in inanimate matter by the action of a force of whose nature we can form no conception. It may perhaps have been a process similar in type to that which later caused the develop-

ment of consciousness in a particular stratum of living matter. The tension which then arose in what had hitherto been an inanimate substance endeavoured to cancel itself out. In this way the first instinct came into being: the instinct to return to the inanimate state. It was still an easy matter at that time for a living substance to die; the course of its life was probably a brief one, whose direction was determined by the chemical structure of the young life. For a long time, perhaps, living substance was thus being constantly created afresh and easily dying, till decisive external influences altered in such a way as to oblige the still surviving substance to diverge ever more widely from its original course of life and to make even more complicated *detours* before reaching its aim of death. These circuitous paths to death, faithfully kept to by the conservative instincts, would thus present us today with the picture of the phenomena of life. If we firmly maintain the exclusively conservative nature of the instincts, we cannot arrive at any other notions as to the origins and aim of life.[2]

After pursuing this line of thought to its extreme, Freud then relativizes it by introducing the idea of another set of instincts to which can be attributed "an internal impulse towards 'progress' and towards higher development!"[3] These are sexual or life instincts. While the death instincts pursue a path of development toward a return to the state of inanimate matter, the sexual instincts "repeat the performance to which [organisms] owe their existence"; that is, they repeat "the beginning process of development."[4]

[The sexual instincts] are conservative in the same sense as the other instincts in that they bring back earlier states of living substance; but they are conservative to a higher degree in that they are peculiarly resistant to external influences; and they are conservative too in another sense in that they preserve life itself for a comparatively long

period. They are the true life instincts. They operate
against the purpose of the other instincts, which leads, by
reason of their function, to death; and this fact indicates
that there is an opposition between them and the other instincts, an opposition whose importance was long ago recognized by the theory of neurosis. It is as though the life of
the organism moved with a vacillating rhythm. One group
of instincts rushes forward so as to reach the final aim of
life as swiftly as possible; but when a particular stage in the
advance has been reached, the other group jerks back to a
certain point to make a fresh start and so prolong the
journey.[5]

Although the life and death instincts oppose one another,
there is a sense in which the partial success of the death instincts facilitates life. Freud asks us to "picture a living organism in its most simplified possible form as an undifferentiated
vesicle of a substance that is susceptible to stimulation."[6] The
outer surface of this vesicle, the surface bordering on the external world, becomes altered when external stimuli impinge
upon it. At some point, the outer surface, permanently
changed by external influences, reaches a limit beyond which
further modification is impossible. "A crust would thus be
formed which would at last have been so thoroughly 'baked
through' by stimulation that it would present the most
favourable possible conditions for the reception of stimuli and
become incapable of any further modification."[7] It is this
"crust" or "shield," this dead zone of organic matter that has
returned to a state of inorganic matter, that both protects the
living substance inside it and makes it possible for that living
matter to have consciousness of the external world. "By its
death," writes Freud,

> the outer layer has saved all the deeper ones from a
> similar fate—unless, that is to say, stimuli reach it which
> are so strong that they break through the protective

shield. *Protection against* stimuli is an almost more important function for the living organism than *reception of*
stimuli. . . . The main purpose of *reception of* stimuli is to
discover the direction and nature of the external stimuli;
and for that it is enough to take small specimens of the external world, to sample it in small quantities.[8]

Stated negatively, the repetition compulsion is an instinctual process of an entirely retrograde nature, a defense against
the vicissitudes of the inorganic world wrought through identification with the inorganic world—organic death. Stated
positively, the repetition compulsion is a post hoc attempt to
thicken the skin, bake the crust, or harden the shield which
protects the life inside. Freud had this latter view in mind
when he suggested that traumatic dreams, dreams that do not
operate in terms of the pleasure principle, "are endeavouring
to master the stimulus retrospectively, by developing the anxiety whose omission was the cause of the traumatic
neurosis."[9]

Nietzsche's Body

When Nietzsche proclaimed that God was dead, he punctured
the "crust" mankind had baked around itself which protected
it from the vicissitudes of the inorganic world. Just as the
outer layer of any living organism is *supposed to be dead* in
order to protect the living organism from excess stimulation
and to provide the limitations necessary if there is to be consciousness, theology is supposed to be dead—rigid, contrived,
defensive, dogmatic—in order to fulfill its function.

Theology stands as a shield between mankind and trauma. A
compromise with the trauma, theology is a return of our ex-
terior surfaces to the inorganic world, that is, to the spiritual
world, death.

To operate optimally, to protect mankind adequately, religion must be a dead shell—mere lip-service, Sabbath after Sabbath, mere duty. The Christianity of Bismarck's Germany, the
Christianity Nietzsche so hated, was a buttress of health and
protection.

But Nietzsche courted higher altitudes and stronger sensations. He was not content with the stimulation that filtered
through the scales and armored plates of Christianity, the
death-in-life religion. He did not want to be a creature deaden-
ing his surfaces in a salvific compromise with the wholly other
creator. He wanted to be a creator in his own right, more fully
than had ever before been dared.

Referring to himself as both "the physiologist" and the "first
psychologist of Christianity," Nietzsche sought to tap the rup-
tures of Christianity's protective shell for a philosophy of the
most intense stimuli. Nietzsche's philosophy is, as he himself
called it, a philosophy of convalescence. In an act of super-
abundant strength, Nietzsche sloughed off his protective
Christian skin and stood exposed before the stimuli that the
dead faith had helped to filter.

Nietzsche was a philosopher of trauma. By renouncing the
benevolent protection of a dead God, he laid himself open to
the "divine influx" of the powers that the dead God helped to
keep at bay precisely through being dead. His personal
ailments—his migraine, his phlegm, his syphilis—he raised to
this meaning.

Nietzsche was forever talking about becoming harder and
colder. His intellect was a robust body which could tolerate
more and more arduous sensations and freedoms. By surrendering his culture's armor of dead theology and exposing
himself to what he called many "little deaths," Nietzsche
sought to become both sensitive and hard at the same time.

In Nietzsche, perception no longer dwelt behind a thick
defensive layer of outer death. The act of perception, for him,
was an aggressive act, an act of willing, inventing and making
that developed its own rugged skin (and renounced it) as it

proceeded. "There are many souls," wrote Nietzsche, "that one will never uncover, unless one invents them first."[10]

The doctrine of eternal recurrence plays the same role in Nietzsche's traumatic philosophy as the repetition compulsion plays in Freud's theory of traumatic neuro-pathology. Just as repetition is a way of retrospectively mastering an overwhelming influx of stimuli by developing the anxiety whose omission caused the traumatic neurosis, eternal recurrence was Nietzsche's way of mastering the stimuli released through his traumatic rejection of Christianity's protective crust—the incarnation and its millennialistic sense of history. By eternalizing every act and moment of his own life, by inflating his every action into the cosmogonic proportions of the original creation, Nietzsche sought to condition himself to the burden of his own existence. Nietzsche felt that if he could commit himself to his every creative act as if it had always been and would always recur, he could replace the protective shield of dead theology with the hard muscle of his own creating will. Eros and thanatos, the life and death instincts, would then no longer be opposed; rather, the two forces would be subsumed under another drive, the will-to-power, the making of one's own life and death and soul.

Sunday Reverie

Sabbath after Sabbath we "act out what we cannot remember" and attempt to "master the [overwhelming] stimulus retrospectively, by developing the anxiety whose omission was the cause of the traumatic neurosis"[11] we call our religion. The job of religion is to fill us with the fear of the Lord—guilt, remorse, sin, anxiety, castration fears—that we might better face the traumas that overwhelmed our ancestors. The faithful are "obliged to *repeat* the repressed material as a contemporary experience [i.e., worship and ritual] instead of, as the physician would prefer to see, *remembering* it as something belonging to the past."[12]

Crust-Making

The tortoise in its shell, the fish in its scales, the rhinoceros in its hide—all creatures great and small—live by virtue of a protective outer crust of dead matter. The purpose of this protective crust or shield, according to Freud, is for "*protection against* stimuli."[13] The shells, scales, skins, and furry hides function as extremely selective perceptual windows or filters, editing out the greater part of the "enormous energies at work in the external world." As Freud writes:

> The main purpose of the *reception* of stimuli is to discover the direction and nature of the external stimuli; and for that it is enough to take small specimens of the external world, to sample it in small quantities.[14]

Soul-making is the human refinement of the crust-making process which is present in all living beings. Human beings, no less than other creatures, are beings with skins, crusts, shells, and hides. I am not just thinking of the history of what mankind has clothed itself in—the animal skins, shirts of mail, hoop skirts, corsets, jock-straps, mini-skirts, polyester suits, designer jeans, space uniforms, and bikini swimwear. I am thinking also of language and metaphor. Men and women live in their metaphors as a tortoise lives in its shell or an animal in its hide. The difference between the person we call "thick-skinned" and the person we call "thin-skinned" may be a function of the ways each dramatizes himself to himself. Whether a potential hurt rolls off us "like water off a duck's back" or flays us alive depends in large measure on the metaphors and analogies we filter it through. To the extent that I can associate the "arrows and slings of outrageous fortune" which befall me to precedents in a text or piece of literature, I will be protected from the raw immensity of that stimulus and, yet, be able to "sample it in small quantities."

Man, in his subtle body, is the most chameleon of all creatures. Faster than the agamid lizard can change its color and disappear against the foliage, the "naked ape," Man, can change his metaphors. The significance of Man's chameleonic capacity becomes clear when we compare him with creatures with extremely thick and inflexible crusts. The oyster, for instance, living on the ocean floor in its rugged shell, is so protected from the stimuli of the external world that the life inside is without a head. Receptive to an extremely narrow band of stimuli, oysters do not see, taste, or smell. Man's capacity to change his skin, shift his metaphors, and wear a variety of garments protects him in a fashion that allows him to sample more of the stimuli transmitted from the external world than any other creature. How unlike an oyster's shell is John Donne's metaphor "like gold to airy thinness beat."

Given that Man owes the evolution of his sentient nervous system to his capacity to protect himself with subtler and subtler skins and linguistic distinctions (metaphors), it is not surprising that in his aesthetics he should value those same qualities. The thinnest porcelain, the most lightweight winter jacket, the slinkiest bikini, the most delicate poem: behind the making of each of these artifacts (though in a restrained fashion) is Shelley's urge to break the imagination's "dome of many-colored glass" to expose "the white radiance of Eternity."

This brings us back to trauma. As a refining of the dead crusts that protect us, soul-making is an attempt to experience more and more of the traumatic stimuli emanating from the world external to us. It is a precarious process of refining sensitivity and perception. Ever and again the temptation is to smash the imagination's dome, go out into the wintry day in too lightweight a coat, or to lie on the sunny beach too long.

Or going the other way, the temptation may be to step up the defensive function of the skin. Today, at a time in history when the United States and the Soviet Union are locked into a reciprocal escalation of paranoid defense activity, the danger for the soul is that the shields may get so thick that closure will result. "Strategic Defense Initiatives" (Reagan's "Star-Wars"), like the rugged shell of an oyster, may well facilitate an atrophying of man's nervous system. Like the oyster in its shell, Man, too, may lose his head.

Like Reagan's S.D.I. program, vicarious religion protects the soul so absolutely from exposure to events that the soul shrivels up for lack of stimulation. The black and white splitting, the reversal of murder into sacrifice and the subsequent identification with the aggressor, the displacement of all tribulation on Christ, the dogma of original sin and its weekly confession—to say nothing of the hysterical conversion reactions—all result in such a blanket response to the challenge of existence that life is sampled in only the most minute dosages.

In what he took to be a "grander system of salvation than the chrystean religion," Keats in his letter to his brother argued for "Soul-making." Soul-making, for Keats, would be the refining of a particularized awareness. Though there may be "sparks of divinity in millions . . . they are not Souls till they acquire identities, till each one is personally itself."

> I[n]telligences are atoms of perception—they know and they see and they are pure, in short, they are God—How then are Souls to be made? How then are these sparks which are God to have identity given them—so as ever to possess a bliss peculiar to each one's individual existence?[15]

Thinner, finer, subtler and more complex: thus does soul want us. The awareness of the particularity of an individual existence is dependent upon relationship with other particulars. But if our skins are so composed that stimuli emanating from another being are leveled out into an amorphous mass of static, or if the skin around the other is similarly constituted, there will exist an insufficient context in terms of which to differentiate uniqueness. The stimuli will continue to be propitiated and preserved at the level of trauma; the "bliss peculiar to each one's individual existence" will not be sensed; the soul will not be made.

Language, Crust, and Deconstruction

Those deconstructionists! What thick skins they have! Imagine the luxury of being able to assert that words are not a function of the objects they seem to signify but, rather, exclusively a function of their relationship to other words. When the psychotherapist reads these critics, he is filled with envy. If only his patients were so linguistically well constituted. If only they could turn their projection-laden, referential communications into self-reflective texts. Like Socrates leading the slave-boy to recollect knowledge he did not know he had, the therapist helps his patients to see the connections between their words, hoping to free them of the blight of referents. If they could only realize that their symptoms are rhetorical, perhaps they would cease vicariously to ascribe blame and salvation to others.

The language spoken by a patient, however, is usually not the language of the text which the deconstructionist reads. The patient's fictions of himself are to literature what prose is to poetry and what life is to death. While the patient's language is a language of *living* referents, literature is elegy, a language of *dead* referents. Poems, plays, and novels, as the deconstructionist critics rightly argue, are never about life. As a layer of dead referents, however, they may serve to protect the life we live in their midst. "This little fragment of living substance," writes Freud, is suspended in the middle of an external world charged with the most powerful energies; and it would be killed by the stimulation emanating from these if it were not provided with a protective shield against stimuli. It acquires the shield in this way: its outermost surface ceases to have the structure proper to living matter, becomes to some degree inorganic and thenceforward functions as a special envelope or membrane resistant to stimuli. In consequence, the energies of the external world are able to pass into the next underlying layers, which have remained living, with only a fragment of their original intensity; and these layers can devote themselves, behind the protective shield, to the reception of the amounts of stimulus which have been allowed through it. By its death, the outer layer has saved all the deeper ones from a similar fate—unless, that is to say, stimuli reach it which are so strong that they break through the protective shield. . . . The protective shield is supplied with its own store of energy and must above all endeavour to preserve the special modes of transformation of energy operating in it against the effects threatened by the enormous energies at work in the external world—effects which tend towards a levelling out of them and hence towards destruction.[16]

The histrionic speech acts of the patient point to the failure of literature. The free-associations, slips of the tongue, and reports of "what happened" are not the ravings of a Lear, the soliloquy of a Hamlet, or the story of an omniscient narrator but, rather, seepage from the fissures in the corpses of these figures. The tragedy of the psychiatric case is the failure of the tragic genre to function as "a special envelope or membrane resistant of stimuli." When a patient's speech is frantic with anxiety, paranoid with referents, or depleted and depressed, it is "a consequence of an extensive breach [having been] made in the protective shield against stimuli."[17]

Those critics who maintain the discontinuity between sign

and signified, word and thing, speak from the robust standpoint of an imperturbably healthy primary narcissism. For them, it is true: inasmuch as they live in the presence of language, inasmuch as their being is a being in soul, there exists no transcendental signified. The psychiatric patient, on the other hand, has a thinner skin. His life has been invaded by an event large enough to wound the narcissism of his protective texts. In the sessions he must speak of it, refer to it, repetitively, compulsively, for, like an anxiety dream, his speech constitutes an endeavor "to master the stimulus retrospectively, by developing the anxiety whose omission was the cause of the traumatic neurosis."[18]

Absence, according to Derrida, is the most compelling form of presence. The insane patient is the amateurish understudy for the absent Lear. The patient, as Freud would say, acts out what he cannot remember, but only to the extent that this also corresponds to what he has not read. Without the protection of an utterly recursive literary imagination, he lies vulnerable and exposed on the heath of his signified, incarnational life. By stumbling around in his role, he attempts to deaden his surfaces in order to fill in the lacuna in the text that should have protected him from the transcendental signified, which, from the purely textual point of view, does not exist. Each fiction and dramatization of the therapy hour is the patient's attempt to thicken his skin with literary crust, whose absence has caused him to be traumatized. By repeating theatrically the trauma of the transcendental signified, the elegy of the overwhelming event, he attempts to cauterize his vulnerability and turn it into the metaphors of an impregnable literature.

Death-Drive and Transference

Whatever traumatizes us we repeat. Whatever we repeat, we repeat with a parent. The repetition compulsion is our filial relationship to an overwhelming event. The repetition compulsion is our death-drive to the parental embrace of the inorganic world. If a collusive counter-transference develops in the therapist, he will enact a death-marriage with the patient. If, however, the therapist is able meticulously to hand back the parental projections, if he is able to abandon the patient's requests for love, while at the same time affirming the portion of life-instincts present in them, the patient will retrospectively develop the protective crust necessary to get on with life.

The repetition compulsion produces a transference around itself as if by incantation. Just as the outer surface of a simple organic vesicle must die and return to inorganic matter so that the stimuli at large in the universe can filter through in a fashion accessible to consciousness, the fierce incest wishes of the transference must die and form a protective shield so that the memories returning from repression can be absorbed into consciousness.

The transference neurosis must be treated before the presenting neurosis in order to ensure that the cure of the presenting neurosis is not vicarious. Before the patient can accept the presenting neurosis as "normal unhappiness," the infantilizing transference projections must be returned. The dead love of the properly handled transference will form a protective skin around the patient making it possible for him to love and work again. "... when a particular stage in the advance [of the death-instincts] has been reached, the other group [of instincts] jerks back to a certain point to make a fresh start...."[19] When the patient is able to dignify the bittersweet intimacy of the therapy by assuming the burden of his or her own life, the therapy has reached a satisfactory conclusion.

Upside-Down

When a trauma has repeated itself many times, it loses its traumatic quality. At a certain point consciousness becomes so saturated with anxiety and reiteration that it can no longer register these events. The compulsive propitiations become automatic; the ritualized avoidances become natural; the neurosis itself becomes comfortable.

When I was a child in school we did a science experiment. One of the students wore a pair of glasses that reversed perception such that the world appeared upside-down. After three days of constantly wearing these glasses and stumbling around in an upside-down world, the boy's perception began to normalize. In spite of the glasses, the world again appeared to him right-side-up. But then, after several days, when the boy took off the glasses, the world appeared upside-down to his naked eyes. He was just as disoriented, nauseous and confused as he was when he had first put on the distorting glasses. It took several days for his perceptual system to adjust and for his picture of the world to turn right-side-up again.

A trauma distorts our perceptions and turns our world upside-down. For a few days, or months, or years we stumble around nauseous and confused. Like the boy wearing the distorting glasses, we become hyper-vigilant. We scan the world for dangers while learning to use our new eyes. Hesitantly, gingerly, reticently, neurotically we walk through the world. (To outsiders all this can look like quite the opposite: staggering carelessness, self-abuse, manic acting-out, histrionic personality disorder.) But gradually our perceptual system accommodates to the traumatic distortion of reality. We become used to the glasses of our negative complexes. The nausea goes away. We find our comfort range. We know where we can go and where we cannot. Our gingerly gait, which is at the same time our staggering gait, comes to feel like our natural gait. Our trauma-skewed perceptions become our home, and we live in them like an agoraphobic, only comfortable when we are "inside" them.

When a chronically neurotic patient, a patient long habituated to his complexed perceptions, complains of anxiety attacks, nausea, or disorientation, it may be because the distorting lenses have been taken off. When the scales fall from our eyes, when the traumatic complexes through which we have been perceiving the world misplace themselves, break, or wear out, the world appears in what seems to be a distorted and threatening aspect. Once we are accustomed to the convoluted perceptions of a traumatized consciousness, situations anomalous to the expectations of that consciousness—benign, non-noxious situations—will seem traumatic. When the patient feels he is getting worse, when he feels a nausea or anxiety that he had not felt for years, it is because he is getting better. The distorting glasses are simply coming off, and the world of mainstream reality returning from repression seems at first upset.

With my patients I sometimes do a countdown. "How many minutes did your anxiety attack last? Five minutes? In the whole week you've had only ten minutes? So in the last ten years you've had only a few days or a week of anxiety, only a few days or a week outside the complex?" When the glasses come off, it takes the patient some time to get used to "real life" again. "This week I want you to have more anxiety attacks if you can possibly manage it. When the glasses come off, leave them off. Don't pick up your bi-focals or your tri-focals. Expect to get a headache, a feeling of dizziness, a feeling of nausea. Make allowances for all that. It will take a while to get over the culture shock of recovery. Give your eyes a chance to adjust."

Transvaluation of All Values

Jesus, it is said, turned the world upside-down. In the Christian dispensation, weakness became valued as strength, slaves replaced their masters and ruled with what Nietzsche, in *The Genealogy of Morals,* called *ressentiment.* Will became anti-will. An aeon of decadence began. "One should not embellish or dress up Christianity," wrote Nietzsche in his book *The Anti-Christ*:

> it has waged *a war to the death* against the *higher* type of man, it has excommunicated all the fundamental instincts of this type, it has distilled evil, the *Evil One,* out of these instincts—the strong human being as the type of reprehensibility, as the "outcast". Christianity has taken the side of everything weak, base, ill-constituted, it has made an ideal out of *opposition* to the preservative instincts of strong life; it has depraved the reason even of the intellectually strongest natures by teaching men to feel the supreme values of intellectuality as sinful, as misleading, as *temptations.* The most deplorable example: the depraving of Pascal, who believed his reason had been depraved by original sin while it had only been depraved by his Christianity![20]

Nietzsche defined Christianity as the "harmful vice" of "active sympathy for the ill-constituted and weak."[21] When looked at through the inverting lenses of Christ crucified, the symptoms of man's weakness became legitimated. The "Good News" of the New Testament was for the poor in spirit. Whatever they could not absorb about themselves, the suffering Christ of vicarious atonement would absorb for them. The weak and afflicted gained an advocacy in the teachings of Jesus. Like diseased sheep huddling together for warmth, Christians enacted what Nietzsche called their "herd morality."

After Jesus turned the world upside-down, Peter, the "rock" upon which Christ built his Church, became the cornerstone of the institutionalization of the Christian inversion of values by asking the Romans to crucify him upside-down. The universal Catholic Church was built from meekness and martyrdom and spread like a disease. As it grew, as it encompassed more and more of the world within its sickly embrace, the agoraphobics living inside it felt less shut in. Soon the soul itself was declared to be naturally Christian.

Nietzsche took off the inverting glasses, the God-glasses, of Christianity and stared down the Christian inversion of reality until it turned right-side-up again. He called his philosophic oeuvre "the transvaluation of all values," by which he meant the subverting of the Christian inversion of truth, in order to return culture to the Greek values of robust health, strength, proportion, and power.

To step out of Judeo-Christianity, to step out of the Great Code as Nietzsche did, is to expose oneself to the dizzying nihilism of an absolute, yet personally discrete, creative freedom. When perception is released from the inverting glasses to which it has so long been accustomed, the world at first seems upside-down and we, perhaps, feel crazy. Weakened by several thousand years of grace, our strength will at first seem clumsy and weak, our reason, hyperbolic and deranged. After walking so long in the flock, we find it difficult to walk on our own two legs again.

Nietzsche recognized this condition and affirmed the strength latent in it when he called himself the philosopher of convalescence. He suffered from blinding migraine headaches, dizziness, nausea, days of vomiting, congenital (?) syphilis, and, later, cerebral paralysis. These enervations were, in his view, strength values of the will returning from the repression (inversion) occasioned by vicarious religion. These symptoms, absorbed into his own soul-making efforts, were the streams which fed the river of his ascending will to power, his *amor fati,* his "yes" to life. Nietzsche's life and death and the vicissitudes he encountered in between were his own. He did not give himself up to vicarious religion. By remaining ever on the side of strength, even when suffering the distress of his own post-Christian body, Nietzsche penetrated out of the Christian inversion of values, the cross of Christ crucified.

Scales off Eyes

When the glasses come off, when one leaves the perceptual field of the traumatic complex, there may be a feeling of guilt, illegitimacy—even criminality.

A middle-aged woman who had been sexually molested by a psychotic relative before the age of five suffered a variety of 'debilitating' phobias, including agoraphobia. With the assistance of a small system of 'helpful' friends, this woman was able to remain shut up inside her house for several decades. This 'upside-down' world was her 'normal' world. So long as she lived in the eye of her trauma, she was quite comfortable and free of anxiety.

But then the inverting glasses began to come off. Several close relatives and several of her helpful friends died. No longer was she able to enlist others to shop for her. No longer did she have a system of people to facilitate her agoraphobia and lend consensus reality to her world. Suddenly, the 'real world' came into focus, although it seemed a topsy-turvy world at first.

The woman turned to psychotherapy for help. Despite an escalation in her level of anxiety, she was able to steal out of her house to come to her individual and group therapy sessions. I say "steal," because entering the world she had so long been disinherited of felt at first like stealing. The patient had long been used to living subversively, in her house, under her rock. She was used to back-doors and back-roads and the ordinances of her phobias.

Whenever there is a trauma, there is a broken covenant in which the psyche festers. The reality principle, having enacted itself too brutally, must give way to the balm of the pleasure principle. While at first the afflicted one may feel illegitimate, bastardly, and disinherited, eventually these feelings come to be replaced by a sense of "squatter's rights." Simply by one's act of surviving, simply by one's act of re-articulating the world through one's fears and avoidances, the disinheritance becomes ontologized. By surviving our abandonment to a traumatic situation, we work out its epistemology. Illegitimacy becomes our legitimacy. Sure-footedly, we walk through the back-alleys of the soul with the instinct of a Kafkaesque dung-beetle and the street-smarts of an orphan in a Dickens novel.

During her treatment, the patient had the following dream:

> I have a job. I am a typist or secretary. The whole cast from my favorite soap-opera are working at the same place, and they are stealing things from the business. The boss is not there right now, and my soap-opera friends are encouraging me to steal too. I'm ashamed to admit it, but in the dream I joined them in the stealing.

The boss who is away may be taken to be the patient's trauma. The soap-opera stars, likewise, may be taken to be the house-gods of her usual agoraphobic universe. For decades the patient has lived inside her trauma, watching soap-operas on television. But here, in this dream, the soap-opera stars and the dream-ego transgress the boundaries of the complex and the rule of the trauma-boss. The patient had recently begun to leave her house and to appropriate ground in the wider world. In therapy she remembered some of the repressed scenes concerning her early childhood molestations. Following the working through of these memories, she took even more freedom for herself. No longer was she living vicariously through the lives of soap-opera stars. With the help of their example and encouragement, she began stealing each day a little more of the world forbidden to her by her old traumatic complexes, until gradually she entered the kingdom that comes like a thief in the night, the kingdom of "normal unhappiness."

4
Homogeneity, Homoeroticism, and Homeopathy

When Two or More Are Gathered Together

The traumatized soul, the soul which cannot make a difference between itself and the overwhelming event which it compulsively repeats, is often best treated in a homogeneous support group. When a patient becomes a member of a group of persons who have been traumatized by a similar event, he or she can begin to make distinctions *within* the event which had previously proven so personally transcending. As each person tells the group what (s)he can about how (s)he was traumatized, each person's trauma gains specificity and particularity.

Jane, Cathy, Margaret and Susan may all use the word "rape" to refer to the trauma they have suffered, but when they hear the discrepancies between each of their assaults they may begin to *experience* the *discrete* proportions of the events they had each been previously unable to relativize. Cathy's date rape and Margaret's gang rape, though both traumatizing assaults, display something of their particularity when compared with each other. When Susan relates how her attacker laughed and wore a mask and Margaret relates how her attacker attempted to strangle her with an electric cord, still more specificity is introduced. As they compare events, the compared events become experiences. Each woman gradually comes to realize that the creature who raped her is not an omnipotent, omniscient and omnipresent God, but in one case a two-hundred-pound trucker with halitosis, in another an economics student from the local college, and in still another case a gang of drunken boys. Each woman must come to realize that the rapist who raped her is not a cosmic rapist and that every rape she reads about in the newspaper is not another of his exploits. In therapy it is crucial to compare details in order to expose the contingent features of a trauma, for if the patient is to make a difference between herself and her trauma she must begin to strip her attacker of the God-like proportions that galvanize her imagination.

Whenever two or more are gathered together in the name of a trauma, the events that had overwhelmed each will be exposed as relative and absorbed into soul. No matter how closely one trauma resembles another and no matter how similar the terms are which we use to refer to them, two of a kind does not exist. There are as many Vietnams as there were men in action, and when the capacity of a veteran to imagine his life forward is dwarfed by events that have staggered his imagination, he must relativize this phenomenon by comparing it with the way war trauma has staggered the imaginations of other veterans.

Although, at first, we may not be able to distinguish between ourselves and an overwhelming event, we can take a first step toward this goal by making distinctions between instances of this inability. How do I differ from what I most resemble? How does my traumatic response differ from the traumatic response of others? How does the event which has overwhelmed me differ from similar events that have overwhelmed others? If we are made in the image and likeness of the trauma which has overwhelmed us, why are we still so different? Why does my traumatization take this particular form and not another?

The homogeneous support group spares each of its members from having to create a relativizing context for his trauma by endlessly repeating it themselves. While, over time, an individual may be able to manufacture a sufficient number of variations on the trauma's theme to relativize the core trauma, the stories of other people with a similar overwhelming event can immediately provide the context through which healing comes. If Jane can have access to the rape stories of Cathy,

Margaret and Susan, her compulsion to generalize the eliciting stimulus of her trauma to other situations in life will be less necessary and less strong. As they tell her what they remember, she will have less need to repeat what she cannot remember and vice versa. The other members of the group, simply by being other, provide a scale of values, a variety of differences. Margaret's gang rape and Susan's near strangulation were the more explicitly violent assaults, but Jane's rape by a man she knew and loved violated more of her sense of trust in even familiar and apparently gentle men. As each woman shares the gruesome details of her own rape, rape becomes particularized in such a way that each woman can differentiate herself from it. Though the proportions of the event had transcended her previous experience and, hence, her previous capacity to make experiences, it may still be seen in proportion when placed in a context of comparable events. By dividing the reified trauma amongst themselves, its victims can strip it of its immeasurable quality, conquer and assimilate it.

Of course, when two or more are gathered together, there is the danger that the group will degenerate into a mere denomination of vicarious religion. If the therapist extracts generalities from the group members' accounts of their traumatization, the cosmic sense of the eliciting stimulus will be preserved. Therapy goes off the track when events that have yet to be experienced and absorbed are pooled together and given a huge name that keeps them quite beyond the reach of precise specification and experience—"post-traumatic stress syndrome," "rape adjustment disorder," "child-abuse." The group members learn the impersonal facts about the trauma they are said to suffer in common. As if reciting a liturgy, the therapist recites statistics from a sociology text. The group is told that a woman is being raped every nine minutes. But whenever "rape," "child-abuse," "Vietnam," or "alcoholism" are spoken of in the abstract, worship is going on.

William Blake, in his critique of organized religion, was very clear on this point. After the "ancient Poets animated all sensible objects with Gods or Geniuses," he writes,

> system was formed, which some took advantage of, & enslav'd the vulgar by attempting to realize or abstract the mental deities from their objects: thus began Priesthood; Choosing forms of worship from poetic tales.[1]

When therapy abstracts "mental deities" or impersonal categories from the minute particularity of events, it loses its poetic basis and substitutes a priestly one. The individual character of the patients' individual stories gets lost as the church fathers of psychology and sociology establish their approved gospel canon of research findings. The cure that comes through particularizing events into experiences, the cure that comes through soul-making, becomes heresy.

The Eucharist of Sexual Assault

The dreamer is a thirty-year-old career woman, wife, and mother. Although she was raised Roman Catholic, she converted to Protestantism while a university student and was later ordained as a minister. The dreams reported here were dreamt at a time when she was working through issues related to the oral rape she had suffered as a twelve-year-old child. For years this trauma had influenced and shaped the dreamer's life in an indirect manner. With the birth of her first child, however, a direct confrontation with the trauma was triggered. The innocence of her newborn daughter reminded her of her own loss of innocence. Out of this crisis she became involved with a local rape crisis center. Working with her trauma and with the challenges this posed for her faith, she gradually began to integrate her understanding of God with her experience of trauma, writing liturgies and prayers for those who had been violated.

About two years after she became a volunteer in the rape crisis center, she had the following dream:

> I am at a large hospital where they have gathered together hundreds of women who have been raped. I go to one doctor upstairs. There is another large room downstairs filled with women where another doctor is treating them. This doctor, I hear, is suctioning all of the sperm out of the raped women. It sounds comforting to me. I feel as though I am part of the group. We have all been raped; but then I have a flashback to my own experience and I feel scared and alone.

This dream images the breakdown of the dreamer's progressive defenses. Although she feels at one with the hundreds of rape victims on the first floor of the hospital, she is, in fact, on the second floor, isolated in a flashback to her own rape scene. The defensive posture of ministering to herself—and then later, as a professional clergyperson, of ministering to others—has isolated her from the sisterhood of women whose soul-making activity together in a homogeneous group helps them to absorb their traumas even as it helps them to draw off the semen which was forced into them. In her life, the dreamer is usually up in a pulpit preaching to a congregation or up on a podium delivering a lecture on sexual violence. Seldom is she simply a 'sister' among 'sisters,' a victim amongst other victims. Up on the second floor of the hospital, up in the pulpit, she is still performing the traumatic fellatio of her childhood—though much less passively now. The *logos spermatikos,* the spermy word of the divine to whose ministry she has been ordained, still bears the traumatic stamp of the oral rape she suffered as a girl. Inasmuch as her sermons and prayers are defenses against the memory of her sexual assault, her rapist is their author.

The movement of the dream as a whole seems to be away from the spirituality of the dream-ego's rape-trauma toward its soulful sorority. Although she cannot yet appreciate it, it is in the flashback to her own rape scene—with all its attendant feelings of aloneness and isolation—that she is more than superficially at one with the other women. It is the progressive defense against these feelings, the adoption of a ministering or missionary posture, that divides her from her sisters.

The next dream (from the same night) explores more fully the tangles among the trauma, the progressive defenses, and religion.

I arrive at a church to hear Marie Fortune speak.[2] As I come in I see Marie dressed in a cool grey alb. I have a good feeling about seeing her again.

The talk about sexual assault and abuse begins. An older man re-enacts how he began to sexually abuse his five-year-old daughter. It is dark and the audience is milling around. We are outside. I see the man find the little girl, who is lying on the table, nude. He begins stroking her leg, then her genitals. This is how it began.

Then we are gathered in an L-shaped room like the downstairs of an old house. I am part of the audience. I want to say something noteworthy. I raise my hand and talk about how the abuse became an erotic obsession, like a religion. If anything I have sympathy for the man, not the girl, in spite of what I heard: that he stuck something through her belly button and inflated her uterus so that the girl's periods began. I think that the girl was disabled after that—some kind of misfit.

When I try to make my intelligent remark, I find that I have a big wad of gum in my mouth so that I can't get my words out. Then I return. The speaker asks me whether I am a nurse. I proudly say that I am a minister.

The talk concludes and I volunteer to drive Marie to the airport since I am going past it to where my mother lives

and is looking after my child. We can't find Marie's alb, and
we look all over the church for it. We still can't find it.
There is some kind of dinner meeting going on.

Religion is concerned with the aspects of existence which
transcend, overwhelm, or traumatize us. If we lived in a world
where events did not exceed our capacity to come to terms
with them immediately and directly, we would have no impulse for religion. Christianity institutionalized an abstract,
generalized relationship to trauma. So abstract and general is
the Church's relationship to trauma, in fact, that we soon
forget that it is based in trauma and see only the actions of a
loving Father, even when that Father is crucifying his only
begotten Son.

But sometimes our individual traumas do not get fully absorbed into the Church's abstract containers. Indeed, sometimes individual traumatic events style our relationship to
religion itself, rendering it idiosyncratic and personal. Though
we all repeat the liturgy in unison, we may each take up the
notion of a transcendent God in terms of the individually specific ways in which we have been transcended and traumatized in our lives. For the minister whose dreams we are
examining, the traumatic model through which she takes up
the notion of a transcendent God was the sexual assault she
suffered at the age of twelve. The man who assaulted her, the
man who dominated her and forced her to perform fellatio on
him, transcended her. Immediately after the attack, her life
became ritualistic and religious. Shadows became charged
with numinosity. She lived constantly with the awareness that
she could again be overwhelmed by transcending spirit, even
if that transcending spirit were only the transcending will of
another attacker.[3]

In the second dream we see that despite the eighteen years
that have elapsed since her rape (or, rather, as a result of
them), religion is still conceptualized in terms of sexual
assault. Standing in for the communion table where matter

was transubstantiated into spirit in the days of her Roman Catholic innocence is the communion table of child sexual abuse where matter is turned into spirit in a fashion closer to her own actual experience. Despite the fact that the man at the altar had "stuck something through [the girl's] belly button and inflated her uterus so that [her] periods began," despite the fact that he aroused the girl's libido before she was old enough to handle it (according to Freud's early seduction theory), the dream-ego finds that her sympathy is with him, the abuser. Wanting to say something "noteworthy," she explains that the man's abusive behavior "became an erotic obsession, like a religion." This is the particular religion of the dreamer. It is the Protestantism to which her sexual assault initiated her and into which she as a minister initiates others.

But the dream takes a turn in another direction. When she tries to make an intelligent remark, she finds that her mouth is filled with a big, sticky wad of gum—a reference to her oral rape (her association). The mouthful of gum in the second dream, like the flashback to the rape scene in the first dream, points to the same thing: the breakdown of her progressive defenses, her identification with the aggressor. To the extent that the dreamer's usual priestly function is upstaged by the high-priest Marie Fortune, to the extent that she finds herself in the congregation amongst the sisterhood of the afflicted, she is tongue-tied by the unassimilated substance of her trauma.

At the end of the dream, "Marie Fortune's" alb (clergy gown) is mislaid and cannot be found. Although the searching dream-ego is still committed to her trauma in its religious dress, the dream as a whole seems to be dislocating the trauma from the priesthood in which it has been robed.

With the loss of the Protestant alb, the dreamer's movement from Roman Catholicism to Protestantism is taken a step further. Protestantism was a protest against priesthood. In Protestantism the gulf between the priest and the laity was narrowed. Each man became his own priest, the celebrant of the mystery of his own trauma, even as our dreamer became a minister herself. Protestantism reclaimed trauma from the priestly exclusivity of Catholicism and allowed a variety of denominational sensitivities and responses. But with the loss of the alb of Protestantism, an even further step is taken. The eucharist of vicarious priesthood de-transubstantiates itself right back into the sticky mouthful of her own personal trauma. Swallowing this sticky mouthful, without the slippery coating of vicarious religion, is what the mystery of "normal unhappiness" is all about.

Judge Schreber's Trauma

Daniel Paul Schreber (b. 1842), the author of the memoirs upon which Freud based his influential paper "Psycho-Analytic Notes upon an Autobiographical Account of a Case of Paranoia (Dementia Paranoides)," was well acquainted with the trauma-God.

> From the first beginnings of my contact with God up to the present day my body has continuously been the object of divine miracles.... Hardly a single limb or organ in my body escaped being temporarily damaged by miracles, nor a single muscle being pulled by miracles.... Even now the miracles which I experience hourly are still of a nature to frighten every other human being to death.[4]

Freud's analysis of the case stresses Schreber's clearly homosexual attitude toward "God" and interprets Schreber's delusions of persecution as a backlash of his having projected his latent homosexual tendencies outside himself. In place of the proposition "I (a man) *love him* (a man)," the paranoiac, according to Freud, substitutes the proposition "I do not *love* him—I *hate* him." This reaction formation is then bolstered by the idea "I do not *love* him—I *hate* him, because HE PERSECUTES ME."[5]

> An internal perception is suppressed, and, instead, its con-
> tent, after undergoing a certain degree of distortion, enters
> consciousness in the form of an external perception. In
> delusions of persecution the distortion consists in a trans-
> formation of affect; what should have been felt internally
> as love is perceived externally as hate.[6]

Freud's analysis, being based solely on Schreber's memoir, is flawed in that the influence of the physical and emotional abuse which the judge suffered as a boy is not considered. But, as Niederland has shown,[7] Schreber's father, an eminent phy- sician and writer on education, held rather sadistic views about child discipline. In several books published on the sub- ject, Schreber senior describes a variety of torturous methods for correcting children. For instance, if a child does not hold his head up straight, the elder Schreber recommended tying the child's hair to its underwear with cords. Likewise, children who do not sit straight in their chairs could be harnessed in a contraption that would press an iron bar into their collarbones should they slouch. To toughen up a child, Schreber's father recommended that infants from the age of three months be washed in cold water.

Niederland's re-examination of the Schreber case suggests that objective correlatives for many of Schreber's persecutory delusions can be found in the sadistic child-rearing prescrip- tions practiced by his father. The traumatizing God of Judge Schreber's memoirs, Niederland's analysis suggests, is none other than the God of his own tortured childhood, his abusive father. This view of Schreber's delusions, Niederland reminds us, is in keeping with Freud's later idea that in hallucinations "something that has been experienced in infancy and then forgotten re-emerges...."[8]

Niederland's re-examination of the Schreber case necessitates a re-examination of the relationship Freud drew between paranoia and repressed homosexuality. If persecutory delusions are derived from traumas and *not* from projected homosexuality, what are we to make of the "homosexual" features in paranoid syndromes? Or, better: if Schreber's paranoia was at bottom a post-traumatic stress disorder, what is the relationship between paranoia, homosexuality and trauma?

Paranoid delusions with a homosexual coloration point to the failure of the *homoerotic imagination* to relativize the overwhelming events which tyrannize over the traumatized soul in a God-like fashion. It is not that paranoia is a projection of literal homosexuality, as Freud argued. Paranoid delusions of homosexual attack are symptomatic of a soul which is afraid of anything metaphorically or homoerotically akin to the original traumatic event. If a trauma has been especially severe, the soul may at first behave as if it were allergic to the cure that comes through likeness. Initially, it may tend to flee from similar events as if they were the overwhelming event. Scanning the environment for signs of the event which had injured it, the soul cannot see the curative forest of resembling events for the immense tree which it is determined not to tangle with ever again. Each likeness that is mistaken for the original trauma, each metaphor that is taken literally, becomes, like the persecutory God of Schreber's delusions, a homosexual attacker. The therapeutic task at this point is to treat the homophobic literalism (the fear of likeness) so that the homoerotic imagination, which will ultimately heal the trauma, can be utilized once more.

Parricide or the Making of Water

The move out of vicarious religion, the move out of the cult of the reified trauma, can be attended by a homoerotic or homosexual ambience. In *Totem and Taboo* Freud associates a homosexual clubbing together of the primordial brothers with the dispatch of their tyrant father.

> Though the brothers had banded together in order to over-come their father, they were all one another's rivals in regard to the women. Each of them would have wished, like his father, to have all the women to himself. The new organization would have collapsed in a struggle of all against all, for none of them was of such over-mastering strength as to be able to take on his father's part with success. Thus the brothers had no alternative, if they were to live together, but—not, perhaps, until they had passed through many dangerous crises—to institute the law against incest, by which they all alike renounced the women whom they desired and who had been their chief motive for despatching their father. In this way they rescued the organization which had made them strong—and which may have been based on homosexual feelings and acts, originating perhaps during the period of their expulsion from the horde.[9]

When the trauma we have learned to call "father" or "God" is stripped of its authority, we become aware of the potency we have collectively projected, as well as the inferiority and inadequacy which these projections had protected us from. Consciousness becomes a double-consciousness, an ambivalence of potency and impotence, power and vulnerability. At this point a homosexual coloration can appear, as we try to sort our individual creative potential out from that of our brothers.

A man who was just in the process of breaking out of the cult of projected creativity and becoming more fully the creator of his own life dreamt that he stood at a urinal in a men's washroom. Around him, crowding him on all sides at nearby urinals, other men were similarly engaged. The dreamer felt uncomfortable at the lack of privacy in this strange men's room and shy at the comparative smallness of his penis. As he tried to push his way out of the crowded washroom, the huge penises of the other men touched him. He felt disgusted, inadequate, lacking in personal boundaries, and defensively superior.

One's own discrete creative power is hard to size up, hard to measure. In a public washroom we stand on our own two feet and make our own living water. There are no vicarious supports or religious containers—except maybe the graffiti written above the urinal to reverse and reify the urinal's estimations.

Imagine Freud, Adler and Jung bumping into each other in some vulgar little washroom after a meeting at a psychoanalytic congress. One can imagine Freud, the atheist, a man self-consciously aware of his own creative power, stoically attempting to master an "unruly homosexual feeling" while peeking over at his colleagues to ascertain whether or not they are circumcised to his—their psychoanalytic father's —will. Adler, meanwhile, we can imagine trying to relax a shy bladder while dreaming up his theory of organ inferiority and over-compensation. (Adler, by the way, later converted from his Jewish faith to Protestant Christianity.) Standing between them is Jung (we imagine), pissing uninhibitedly, loud and long, the devotee and favorite of the God who shat upon the Basel cathedral in his childhood dream.[10]

Freud struggled with a greater burden of homosexual feelings than Jung did because he saw religion as an illusion whereas Jung did not. When relationship matters were addressed in their letters, Jung confessed to Freud that he had an ambivalent "'religious' crush"[11] on him, whose traumatic model was the sexual abuse he suffered as a child at the hands of a man he had idolized.[12] Unable to face the intimacy of their creative equality with all its homoerotic sorting out, Jung chose to project his creativity into the worship of Freud. He protected himself from equality by styling himself as Freud's son, only to later disparage the inequality and berate Freud as a tyrant. Of course, Freud's overly literal conception of homoerotic feelings didn't help the situation. Freud shrank away from an equal relationship into materialistic propitiations of the homoerotic feelings no less than Jung shrank from them into spiritualized avoidances.

As great as the accomplishments of Freud and Jung have been as the founders of rival viewpoints, their achievements fell far short of the possibilities available to them had they been able to cooperate. Constellated in the relationship between them was the psychic energy pent-up for millennia in the supernatural containers of their Hebrew-Christian culture. In the early years of this century, psychoanalysis was pregnant with the total renewal of culture. But the pregnancy was aborted. Unable to work through the homoerotic transference reactions between them, Freud and Jung parted ways.

A man, whose decision to enter Jungian analysis reflected a movement out of vicarious religion into the active making of his own psychology, dreamt that he was in his parents' backyard. The huge tree that had dominated the yard had been cut down, reduced to a stump. Throughout the yard, the roots of the felled tree sent up shoots by the hundreds. The shoots, it seemed, were penises.

This dream, like the men's washroom dream, images the multiplication of penises that accompanies the renunciation of vicarious religion and the restoration of creative power to man. The two dreams reflect a psychology that has begun to penetrate out of the covenant of circumcision. Penetrating out of the covenant of circumcision means penetrating out of the religious assurances that God will make of us a great nation. It means standing at one's own little urinal, no longer allowing the conjectures of Abraham's penis to reach beyond the discrete possibilities of one's own. It means killing both the totem and the taboo.

The female side of all this Freud termed "penis envy." This concept is a materialized recognition of the struggle women have had assessing their potency in a male-dominated world. If it has been hard for men to stand at the urinal of their own creative destiny, it has been harder still for women. Fortunately, women have more and more become able to release themselves from their so-called penis envy and assume responsibility for their own creativity. No longer do they conceive of themselves as the concubines of the circumcised. Following in the footsteps of their female peers, men, too, are beginning to penetrate out of the penis envy which circumcision (i.e., the covenantal relationship with the vicarious phallus of a creator-god) has locked them into.

Archetypal Psychology

James Hillman's move from the noumenal archetype to the archetypal or phenomenal image[13] is a Jungian compromise with Freud's clinical mythology. The noumenal archetype has dominated Jungian thought like the tyrant father of Freud's *Totem and Taboo,* leading at times to ham-handed interpretations. In the writings of James Hillman the images have banded together as brothers, killed the abstract archetype and eaten it. Like the father in the belly of his sons, "the archetype," writes Hillman, "is wholly immanent to its image."[14] The incest taboo comes into play with the same move that affirms the totem substitute: just as the brothers, according to Freud, renounced their desire to take possession of all the women—an act that would imprison the anima once more in a father's testicles—the archetypal school makes monotheism taboo. No single perspective, no one brother, may dominate the psyche and hoard the multiple possibilities of soul.

Lesbian Grounding

A middle-aged woman artist who was just becoming aware of her tendency to project her creative power on men—accepting them as sexual partners or rejecting them accordingly—had the following dream:

> I am making love to an unknown woman. Our bodies form a perfect circle. Two vague, unknown men watch us. Apparently we are going to make love to them after we finish. The room we are in has only two walls (forming together a single corner). Behind the wall a vague, unknown woman is walking. We do not have sex with them.

The lesbian love-making and the unacted desire to make love to the men are precisions of the same image. The dream-ego makes love to her own sex precisely by not getting around to having sex with the men who watch nearby, and vice versa. The dreamer's heteroerotic tendency to project her creativity on men in sexual relationships has become contained in lesbian embraces. The women perform cunnilingus on each other, their bodies forming a perfect circle. The dreamer's creative power is contained in its own feminine orbits. Although men are near and desirable, the dream-ego does not short-circuit her creative power through them.

The room has two walls that form a single corner. Behind the wall walks a vague, unknown woman. Is this the old feminine tendency? Is this the woman who would project her creative power on men, making love to them without adequate lesbian grounding? Or is this the feminine creative principle returning from repression? I suppose it all depends on whether the dreamer can sustain her homoerotic stance or not.

A traumatic model for the surrender of feminine creative power to men is the primal scene. According to Freud, a child's first impressions of sexuality give rise to a "sadistic conception of coitus."[15] The child sees its father on top of its mother; it hears the moans and cries of coitus and believes that the father is beating the mother. When the child discovers that its mother lacks a penis while the father possesses one, the fantasy is formed that the father castrated her. If the child is a girl, she may believe that her father castrated her as well. If this happens, the girl will tend to resent her mother for not protecting her and will form an affectionate tie to the father who she feels could hurt her again.

In the artist's dream, the primal scene is being absorbed into soul. Although at first the women may possibly be licking each other's vagina as if they were licking a castration wound, they are also mirroring each other, providing each other the homoerotic field of comparison necessary to bring into consciousness a wholly feminine conception of their creative power. If the dreamer is able to resist emasculating herself with the old mythology, if she is able to resist enlisting a man to be the carrier of her creative power, the lesbian cunnilingus will perhaps obtain this emancipating meaning.

Homoerotic Imagination

The imagination tends to operate in terms of resemblances, likenesses, sames. One story leads to another story leads to another. We perceive things *homoerotically* in terms of brotherhoods and sisterhoods. We individuate objects and events into unique shapes by noticing how they differ from what they most resemble.

This homoerotic style of imagination, this attraction of like for like, is as natural as our own sensations. The smell of today's roses calls into play the absent roses, the roses of yesterday. The nose constructs their smell by an act of deconstruction. I smell my sensations by comparing them with my repressed sensations, the subtext, the latent homoerotic brotherhood of resembling sensations in memory. I smell the *difference*. But this natural bent or primary narcissism of mind, this play of resonance and resemblance, can be short-circuited by trauma.

An overwhelming event, an event for which we cannot find a field of comparison (and, therefore, cannot fully experience and absorb), is traumatic. A trauma is anything we can't talk about in a Platonic dialogue. It is whatever we have a dogmatic relationship with or consider too sacred to blaspheme. It is whatever we cannot entertain as a fiction because we have turned it into a religion. Trauma polarizes consciousness into opposites—black and white, male and female, pleasure and unpleasure. Heteroerotic imagination, the imaginational mode of the antithetical and opposite, has its source in trauma. An overwhelming event, an event which cannot be contained for lack of analogies, traumatizes and polarizes the mind. Something frightens or hurts us. We flee from it, but as we do so it becomes more frightening. As matters escalate and greater and greater tensions develop between the opposites, the trauma repeats itself. Because of its heteroerotic effects on the imagination, traumata are able to reproduce themselves in the mind.

To break out of the heteroerotic trauma cycle we need to enter the homoerotic mind. Like cures like. Our traumas can be healed by conversations and dialogues. Homogeneous support groups—groups for alcoholics, groups for battered wives, groups for incest survivors and sex offenders, etc.—are medicinal. We can only turn an overwhelming event into an absorbable experience by comparing it with other resembling events. Together we can compare notes and read the larger subtext in terms of which we can locate ourselves uniquely, particularly, discretely.

Trauma Anonymous

If whatever we do once is a trauma (for lack of a field of comparison), whatever we do twice is a ritual, a religion. Twice, three times, four, five—all numbers greater than one are an attempt to incorporate the first time, the number one.

The first cut is the deepest. One is always the biggest number. Jung even said that it is a fictive ideal and that the first real number is two.[16]

The variegated imaginal field, the ten thousand things of the soul, the petit observances and obsessive compulsions of our day to day routines multiply and multiply again as if trying to engulf and incorporate the original fiat, the number one, the first time.

Mathematically speaking, the soul-making process is limitless. One event requires a second to give it a context as an experience. The second event then requires a third, the third a fourth, and so on ad infinitum. All arithmetic is the festering exegesis of the unfathomable number, the number one.

The alcoholic, according to the popular adage, begins with his first drink; however, it would take a master of a not yet invented psychoanalytic calculus to measure the acceleration from that first drink to the second and to the last. Perhaps addiction is paradoxically an attempt to experience rather than an attempt to escape experience. Perhaps what locks the addict into the addiction is that in his repetitive bouts of substance abuse he is trying to *experience* his original 'anti-experience' with the drug. From this perspective, each successive black-out is an attempt to remember and experience the first black-out. It is an obsession with the missing time, the forgotten hours, the spirit of absence that drives the addict. He gets high not in order to lose himself in a fresh state of oblivion, but, rather, to re-enter the original oblivion in the hope that he might find himself, the hours of himself that he has lost. It is not only that the chemicals addict physiologically. By depressing the nervous system and diminishing consciousness, the alcohol renders the cyclical process by which consciousness is made a game without end. The alcoholic's downward spiral is also an infinite regress. By means of his second full bottle he searches for his first empty. But when he returns to his origins, he does not see them as if for the first time. No sooner has he absorbed the substance of his trauma than he passes out again.

Reading and Writing

Reading can be traumatic. It may take years for a student to take in what he reads. The material is at first too overwhelming. Hegel—what? Dostoevsky—what? Marx—what? In essays and assignments the student repeats the trauma of his reading, paragraph after paragraph. He consults the experts and reads the study guides as if trying to develop in retrospect the pedantic anxiety or pedantic crust, whose lack occasioned his trauma in the first place. The student needs the repressed texts in order to assimilate the traumatic text. Reading comprehension proceeds by indirection. An understanding gradually coagulates when enough of the homoerotic field of comparison has been read. The trauma of one book supplies the subtext for another, and one trauma cancels out another.

5
The Trauma of Incarnation
and
the Sur-Natural Soul

Why and Because

Perhaps the most basic trauma of all is the trauma of *incarnation*. By *incarnation* I do not mean the vicissitudes a baby suffers while navigating the birth-canal—the so-called birth-trauma of Otto Rank. I mean, rather, the overwhelming nature of our given reality. The doctor may count up our fingers and toes when we are born, but even if he pronounces that we are all there, the *form* of our existence is, nonetheless, irrational and arbitrary. "Why five fingers? Why not six? Why do we need to defecate, to procreate, to eat? Why Mommy? Why? Why?"

Perhaps humanity can be divided into two groups: the group that are satisfied by the tautological reply "because" and the group that are not.

The first group, the group that easily adjusts to the arbitrary, irrational character of existence, is typically perceived to be the most natural and healthy. Although, objectively speaking, their lives are simply a collection of irrationalities, they can experience their existence as rational, so long as its irrationality is congruent with the irrationality of the world itself. Existential conflicts do not occur to these cast-iron constitutions. As children they grow like weeds; as adults they succeed in the world; as parents they answer every "why?" with "because."As each successive generation grows up as unconscious as the last, the *congruence* within this transgenerational transmission process of anti-awareness paradoxically lends the illusion of consciousness, meaning and purpose to life. But when the preservation of the species, the cycle of biology, and the universal repetition of the Oedipus-complex suffice as the meaning of life, the "because" has triumphed.

The second group, the group of people less identified with the hazard of their incarnational life, the group who cannot be reconciled to the irrationality of existence by an amused "because," are typically perceived as being more or less neurotic. The given world never quite makes sense to these people. Eating, drinking, defecating, and procreating seem, at best, a servitude to the irrational. The question "why" continues to be an obsession, perhaps even distorting itself into a case of hypochondria or paranoid character. With their 'peculiar' behavior and 'neurotic' reticence, this second group seem 'irrational' to the radiant members of the first group who are so absorbed into the arbitrariness of existence that it no longer seems the least bit illogical to them. (From the point of view of the second group, the members of the first group seem brutish, vulgar, insensitive and callously vital.)

Between the two groups there is an exchange of traffic. It frequently happens, for instance, that a member of the first group can fall from his pristine grace into the company of his less happily incarnated brothers. Perhaps some overwhelming event befalls him from some irrational quarter, disinheriting him of the world which had previously seemed so straightforward and true. Perhaps he sustains an injury or contracts an incurable disease. Perhaps a parent dies or his family is divided by a divorce. "Why me?" he cries; "Why me?", but no longer can a "because" serve as a magic answer.

Traffic going the other direction often proceeds by means of the consolations of religion. Those souls who feel like strangers in a strange land—"in this world, but not of it"—often find in the illusions of religion sufficient rationale to make the absurdity of the world stomachable.

But is there not another answer to the soul's "why" than the "because" of nature and the "because" of religion? There is. This other option is re-creation, culture-making, soul-making.

The act of re-creation, the act of giving our own form to the chaos of existence, takes us out of the traumatic parent/child rhetoric of "why" and "because."

If we think of this in isolation it seems all too heroic: every person an originating artist. What I have in mind when I speak of soul-making, however, is the *re-engagement of culture*. For some, soul-making may indeed mean originating; for most people, however, it means giving the developments of culture their psychological assent—claiming the changes, evaluating them and instinctualizing them accordingly. Today we live in the dispensation of a long history of other makers. The "whys" and "becauses" that once punctuated the traumatic absurdity of existence have been increasingly absorbed into the free verse of man's own creating will.

After Jesus told his disciples that "it is easier for a camel to go through the eye of a needle, than for a rich man to enter the kingdom of God," Peter replied, "Behold, we have left everything and followed You; what then will there be for us?" Jesus answered Peter's question by promising that "you who have followed Me, in the regeneration when the Son of Man will sit of His glorious throne, you also shall sit upon thrones judging the twelve tribes of Israel":

> And everyone who has left houses or brothers or sisters or father or mother or children or farms for My name's sake, shall receive many times as much, and shall inherit eternal life.
>
> But many who are first will be last; and the last, first. (Matthew 19 : 24, 27-30)

If we read this passage gnostically, taking the promise of inheriting eternal life to mean the tapping of our age-old cultural inheritance, we discover a curious relationship between absence and presence. Again and again biography places before us examples of lives in which the first have become last, where the second born succeeded the first, where the needle's eye of inheritance was disinheritance.

The absurd event we take for granted as members of the first group enters the mind as a content of consciousness, or the soul as an experience, only when we lose our unquestioning grip upon it. When we fall into the second group, the group of the dispossessed, what we have lost becomes immensely present in its absence. The dead parent, the lost love, the faded beauty—precisely by virtue of being dead, lost, and faded—are released from their literal encasement in the absurd and become metaphors. Although still particular, they 'float' as categories, perspectives, integrities of soul, intelligences, angels. Trauma is the eye of the needle through which we enter the kingdom of culture. Through the thorns in our flesh we re-engage culture, body it forth anew, evaluate and instinctualize it.

The boy without a father, for example, can be fathered by the culture. Through the eye of his wound he can see a variety of fathering forms, most of which are entirely invisible to the boy of the first group who plays ball after supper with a man whose genetic resemblance to him masks the arbitrariness of the whole human enterprise. (This arbitrariness is the basis of creative freedom, and so to really be granted awareness of it is the blessing of the absent father.) The boy without a father tends to become a phenomenologist of fathering. He watches television programs, reads books, evaluates his mother's lovers and the fathers and step-fathers of other boys. Perhaps he breaks windows and commits crimes. In any case, he finds presence through the needle's eye of its absence. His inheritance is a subtle inheritance: the experience of "fathering" as an event of the soul—discontinuous, yes, but ubiquitous for all that.

Arbitrary Particulars

Wordsworth knew about arbitrary particulars and what acceptance of them in a *determinate* sense cost. He knew how quickly the soul, given over to events it is unable to alter, becomes dislocated from its imaginal power. In his poems Wordsworth poignantly described the insidious process by which the play of the mind becomes restricted by the brute circumstances which were given with its birth.

> And the Babe leaps on his Mother's arm—
>> I hear, I hear, with joy I hear!
>> —But there's a Tree, of many, one,
> A single Field which I have looked upon,
> Both of them speak of something that is gone:
>> The Pansy at my feet
>> Doth the same tale repeat:
> Whither is fled the visionary gleam?
> Where is it now, the glory and the dream?[1]

The arbitrary particulars of our incarnational life traumatize awareness. The sheer concreteness and outwardness of existence upstage the "visionary gleam … the glory and the dream." Each particular thing that we arbitrarily encounter commits us to the objective sphere in a manner which has a determining effect upon all subsequent encounters. As Freud and Breuer put it, "any impression which the nervous system has difficulty dealing with by means of associative thinking or by motor reaction becomes a psychical trauma."[2]

Life itself is traumatic to soul. Simply by virtue of becoming actually something or someone to somebody, the soul ceases to be potentially anything and everything to anyone and everybody. Predicated to the few which make up its actual life, the soul loses sight of its immortal attributes and becomes a function of the lowest terms it holds in common with the other beings with which it shares life's stage. But this deadly prose of incarnation can give way to poetry. Though "our birth," as Wordsworth writes, "is but a sleep and a forgetting," it is still possible to explore while 'sleeping'—through a dream, a verse, or a poem—what incarnation requires the soul to forget. Though our lives are ultimately embedded in circumstances beyond our power to alter, *we can still imagine.* Imaginal modes such as poetry provide the soul with access to the psychic potentialities which incarnation into the actualities of life would otherwise have caused it to relinquish.

Chronicity

Sometimes we cling to a particular trauma precisely because it individuates us from the trauma of particularity, the trauma of arbitrariness, the trauma of incarnation. Although a trauma could be absorbed, it often lingers on in the form of intractable symptoms that seem grounded in an even more intractable attitude. Rather than allow our trauma to be absorbed into the existing categories of assimilation (given, in part, by our family mythology), we obstinately align ourselves with it in order to call into question our ordinary method of turning events into experiences. In an effort to re-locate our arbitrary categories of assimilation, we dig in our heels and resist recovery. It is as if we cling to a trauma because the soul wants the "why?" it raises. To allow the trauma to be too easily assimilated would only be to swallow it with the sugar coating of a "because," and to the Gnostic sensibility the metaphysical consolation of a "because" merely adds insult to injury.

We are arriving at a paradoxical formulation. While we have

been defining trauma throughout this book as an overwhelming, unabsorbable event, now we are suggesting that a trauma can also open consciousness. Partly, what a trauma confers on us is a sense of individuality. Something has happened to us that makes us unlike anyone else we know. Often it is less the specific calamity that we cannot absorb—the rape, the acne, the abuse, the accident—it is the *individuality* these events underline and particularize us into.

In a deep sense the individuality of the soul is always unabsorbable. After all, it is not the soul that we absorb; it is the soul that does the absorbing. When a trauma resists absorption, it is because in a deeper sense the soul is resisting incarnation, a "why?" is resisting a "because." It is not just that the trauma overwhelms the categories of assimilation with which the soul tries to incorporate it. The corollary is also true: the soul is overwhelmed with itself, with its own particular character structure. It is as if we individuate a relationship to the sur-natural soul by chronically refusing the consolations of the only-natural order. The traumatized soul is as well self-traumatizing. Inasmuch as it, too, is arbitrary, it is a trauma to itself. Ultimately, a trauma is as unabsorbable as the soul, according to Heraclitus, is bottomlessly deep. Like the Gnostic before his angel, the soul before its trauma is made a stranger to itself. This is its initiation into gnosis.

Refusing Incarnation

Symptoms are arbitrary particulars dis-incarnating themselves from their encasement in the arbitrary order of the simply given world. Phobias, eating disorders, sexual dysfunctions, etc.: in all these conditions the natural or "normal" state of our being has been disrupted. Behaviors that were once simply spontaneous aspects of our arbitrary animality become self-conscious, reflective, inhibited objects of concern and worry. It is as if by losing our capacity to maintain an erection, experience an orgasm, eat food, or walk in the marketplace, etc., that we become human. When the monkey lost its tail and fell out of its tree, it stood up and became Man.

We regain what we lose only by re-creating it. After we experience the failure of what had hitherto functioned automatically and unconsciously, we can never again take it for granted. With the development of a symptom innocence is lost. The penis will not erect again until we re-invent it. No matter how hard the patient tries, he cannot will back its old spontaneity. But if he takes his lead from the symptomatic state of his penis, he can penetrate out of its old mythology precisely by means of its flaccidity. As the penis is re-invented (by changing the feelings and attitudes surrounding it), it loses its arbitrary animality and becomes part of human intercourse. Now, paradoxically, the spontaneity can return, at least until the possibilities of the new mythology have been exhausted. In our soul-making we need never fear: a recurrence can always happen should we need a new orientation.

The Fallacy of Susceptibility

Other writers have written about trauma, but invariably their focus has been to describe trauma from the limited standpoint of life situations believed to be particularly susceptible to traumatic effects. Trauma has been discussed in terms of birth (Otto Rank, Arthur Janov), childhood sexual assault (early Freud), overwhelming drive impulses and fantasies (the later Freud), world-shaking cataclysms such as earthquakes, floods and solar eclipses (Immanuel Velikovsky), family communication (Laing, Esterson, Cooper, Bateson, Weakland), insensitive parenting and "poisonous pedagogy" (Alice Miller). But the principle *pars par toto* does not apply to trauma. No single susceptibility has a monopoly on trauma. In fact, I question the very notion of *susceptibility*. Trauma, at least as I have come to define it, is simply that which is overwhelming and determining. Birth, childhood, family, sexuality, instinctual drives and the physical states of the planet are not mere areas of traumatic susceptibility; inasmuch as they are the inexorable conditions of existence they *are* the trauma.

The notion of susceptibility suggests that some foreign body impinges destructively on some natural situation of our being. But in a deeper sense the opposite is the case. It is the 'natural' and so-called 'susceptible' situations that impinge on the unnatural soul. Yes, that's right: soul is unnatural or, as the alchemists said, an *opus contra naturam,* a work against nature into culture.

Anything natural is traumatic to soul. The simply given is overwhelmingly arbitrary. Deeper than what my parents may or may not have done to me is the absurd fact that I was born to these particular individuals. Trauma exists *a priori.* It resides in the sheer arbitrariness of our particular existence. That parents and children abuse each other is, at least in part, the simple extension of the fact that the soul does not recognize biological ties as necessary. Why was I born to these parents and not to others? Why was I born to peasants? Why did we have a girl? I wanted a boy. (Sentiments of deep resignation—e.g., "I can't do it, I'm only a woman"—are often simply reversals of the soul's basic incredulity before mere being.) As Wordsworth put it:

> . . . even with something of a Mother's mind,
>   And no unworthy aim,
>   The homely Nurse doth all she can
> To make her foster child, her Inmate Man,
>   Forget the glories he hath known,
> And the imperial palace whence he came.[3]

The notion of susceptibility promotes vicarious thinking. There is little difference between designating God's only begotten Son as so particularly susceptible to trauma that he can take on the trauma of the whole world, on the one hand, and designating birth, early childhood, family process, or anything else as especially vulnerable and therefore sacred on the other. The analysis of the past can be as vicarious as the wor-shiping of Christ crucified. Whatever we hold to be holy—birth, childhood, family, innocence, sexuality, fantasy—we preserve at the level of trauma by the simple act of hallowing it.

It is not that child-abuse and other events are not important problems. They are. We abuse our recognition of child-abuse, however, when we assign it the lion's share of etiological significance. Rather than absorbing the events from these quarters, we turn them into cult reactions replete with sow's ears and indulgences. Believing in the extreme vulnerability of one place in life requires us to overcompensate in another. Now as crusading missionaries (social workers, psychologists, super-parents), we potentiate and facilitate exactly what we propitiate, though now with a clear conscience, our virtue hav-ing already paid for our vice.

All neurosis is traumatic neurosis. Neurotic consciousness is a consciousness narrowed by the events it has not yet ade-quately experienced. There is nothing abnormal about this. We must expect there to be a discrepancy between an event and the experiencing of it. Perhaps when we stop conceiving of trauma as damage we will stop conceiving of neurosis as sick or wrong and vice versa.

This brings us to the other side of the trauma = damage coin: health. We posit an optimum state of well-being against which to measure our damage and model our recovery. Just as God has become a whitewashed, reified version of the events we cannot experience and absorb, health is the whitewashed, reified version of our so-called ills. Unable to be sick, unable to convalesce and experience what is happening for us, we do a flip and try to be healthy. (The reverse situation also occurs.) But from the point of view of the soul, we are just as 'sick' when we are 'healthy' as when we are 'ill.' For unless the soul has been touched, recovery and illness may be merely flights into each other.

Seduction Fantasies

A trauma does not *cause* a psychological effect like one snooker ball transferring its motion to another. When the psyche changes its metaphors, the cue ball or traumatic stimulus may vanish altogether. In the soul-making process, the terms of reference through which events are experienced may change such that a specific trauma is no longer in play on the same table of values. We must not let "trauma" become a vicarious concept, blaming it for our psychic ailments, as if the psyche were something whole and immaculate that is simply there to be chipped away on—bruised, molested, abused. Soul makes itself out of trauma and in the process can be at least as aggressive as the content it incorporates. In a sense soul wants to be opened, twisted, shocked, abused, stimulated. Perhaps what Freud asserted about children when he formulated his theory of infantile sexuality could be more correctly asserted about the soul. After all, soul (not children) has its seduction fantasies, calling Eros down upon it for what Plato and Blake called "generation."

A Child Is Being Beaten

Yes, but what about the abused child? What about the child whose parent so cruelly molested it and who now has five personalities?

If even those of us born with every possible advantage question the arbitrariness of mere being, all the more do those who experience arbitrariness in the form of violence and exploita-tion question it. "Why do I have to stay home and do secret things with Daddy when the other kids get to play together?" For the abused child, childhood is less a Wordsworthian ode on intimations of immortality than it is an intimidation of im-mortality. And, yet, the hysterical symptoms could be con-sidered to be the soul dancing and could be celebrated as such if it were not that the dance was being forced by the bullets of abuse being fired at its feet.

But still, for all this, I see the formulation of bizarre and im-aginative symptoms to be less a sign of the tragedy of child-abuse than a hope for its remedy. The last can become first. Where an incarnational life has been rendered impossible, a psychic life may have its span. Unable to be the child of a par-ticular parent, one may instead become a child of the culture, a daughter of the Jerusalem of her own creative survival, a Son of Man, a metaphor. Yes, perhaps if there were more meta-phors around, there would be less abuse.

Traumatology

Metapsychologies, the extra-psychic assumptions and conjec-tures upon which a psychology rests, are traumatologies. The prefix *meta* applied to the word *psychology* gives the meaning "like psychology, but not psychology." Thus, metapsychol-ogies are attempts to give an account of the events which af-fect psychic life, but which have yet to be absorbed by the psyche, made into soul.

Theories are forms of prediction, propitiation, even magic. Given the traumatic content which theories try to propitiate, we need not wonder that metapsychological concepts can be-come dogmatic—totem and taboo. A psychology worthy of its own salt must be first and foremost a trauma to itself. Only by confronting the trauma which its metapsychological conjectures seem to cover can a psychology stay psychological. Too easily the psyche gets absorbed into matter or spirit. Metapsychological assumptions tend to make the psyche a function of something believed to be more substantially real—brain chemistry, instincts, psychodynamics, archetypes, deity.

Strange that psychology must always take a backseat to itself, placing more value upon what it hasn't experienced than upon what it has. Partly, I suppose, this is what keeps psychology a process. If psychology did confer on itself a higher value, it might fall victim to a kind of aesthetic sentimentalism, an idolatrous worshiping of its own experiences, that would close down its process and prevent further experiences. Psychology would become spirit by contemplating its own navel.

The relegation of psychic reality to a position 'inferior' to other modes of being wounds psychology's narcissism just enough to keep it ever open and ever opening. So although metapsychologies are anti-psychological, perhaps we can imagine them as links which connect us to the places where we are still not psychological.

As long as there is a turnover of theories and assumptions, we can be sure that our psychology-making is a work of soul-making. The prefix *meta,* applied to psychology, means that psychology is always negating itself so as to open itself. As an endless process of confronting its own tendency to closure, psychology is *meta*—like itself, but never quite, and, yet, always metaphorical.

Gnostic Transference

If the soul is 'unnatural,' a perennial "why?" before the arbitrariness of mere being, what are the 'occult' contents of the transference? In the Freudian view, the contents of the transference are the parental imagos. The patient transfers his or her parental complexes to the therapist, and a therapy of re-parenting or de-parenting is then conducted according to the therapist's inclinations. But from a Gnostic, Platonic, alchemical or Wordsworthian point of view, what is projected on the therapist in the transference is the naturalistic fallacy into which the soul has been incarnated. By projecting the arbitrary particularity of his incarnational life on the person of the therapist, the patient converts those fettering particulars into metaphors. It is precisely because the therapist is not the patient's mother or father that the patient can penetrate out of his mother and father by projecting their particularity on him. In the transference, the parental imagos shed their historical sense of particularity (the therapist is, after all, patently *not* the historical parent) and 'float' as categories, just as they did when as a young child the patient could still wonder why he was born to his parents and not to others.

In the wrangles of the transference, it is not simply the specific infantile wishes and the specific disappointments that the patient works through. It is the whole problem of incarnation that he confronts. The fierce incest wishes of the transference, the oral aggressiveness and oral greed are a form of *via negativa*. It is not that the 'natural' child is continuing in the adult patient to make infantile demands of the parent whom he projects on the therapist; it is, rather, that the 'unnatural soul' is negating the determinate status of the particularity in which it is trapped, exposing this as arbitrary and absurd. When the patient can see as arbitrary the things he once had seen as determinate, and when he can wed this resultant sense of Maya to his own creating will, the provisional (vicarious) life is over.

A therapy which aims at soul-making takes the side of the 'sur-natural' soul. Its sensibility is like that of Wordsworth when he wrote in his "Ode: Intimations of Immortality":

Of Childhood, whether busy or at rest,
With new-fledged hope still fluttering in his breast—

Not for these I raise
　　The song of thanks and praise;
　　But for those obstinate questionings
　　Of sense and outward things,
　　Fallings from us, vanishings;
　　Blank misgivings of a Creature
Moving about in worlds not realized [i.e., not seeming
　　real]
High instincts before which our mortal Nature
Did tremble like a guilty Thing surprised;
　　　But for those first affections,
　　　Those stormy recollections,
　　Which, be they what they may,
Are yet the fountain of light of all our day,
Are yet master light of all our seeing;
　　Uphold us, cherish, and have power to make
Our noisy years seem moments in the being
Of the eternal Silence: truths that wake,
　　　To perish never;
Which neither listlessness, nor mad endeavor,
　　　Nor all that is at enmity with joy,
Can utterly abolish or destroy![4]

Therapy, from this point of view, is a recollection of the so-called archetypes of the collective unconscious or, more simply, a re-engagement of culture.

At this point not Freud, but Norman O. Brown and C. G. Jung become our masters. While Freud's psychoanalytic ambition was abbreviated into the famous dictum "Where id was, there shall ego be. It is reclamation work, not unlike the draining of the Zuider Zee,"[5] Brown affirmed the corollary: where ego was, there id shall be. Jung, too, took the side of the polymorphously perverse child of the id, the side of the 'unnatural' or 'sur-natural' soul, with his theory that beyond the particularity of the personal unconscious lay the archetypes of the collective unconscious, and with his clinical finding that if transference is allowed to elaborate itself freely anything (i.e., a multitude of trans-particular collective contents) can be transferred.

Phone Home!

In recent years extra-terrestrial fantasy films have pro-liferated—*E.T., Cocoon, Starman,* etc. The appeal of these films, I believe, lies in the nostalgia they touch in us for the non-arbitrary form of the subtle body or 'sur-natural' soul. The extra-terrestrial life forms portrayed in these films, with their strange organs and unique appendages, resonate with the part of us that once wondered, "Why do I have five fingers and not six or three? Why was I born into these particular circum-stances?"

Perhaps, one day, Steven Spielberg will be recognized as a father of psychoanalysis. Alongside Anna O. and the Wolfman we will one day place his film *E.T.,* regarding it as a great case in the history of the science (fiction) of soul.

Imagine that the patient in analysis is E.T., the extra-terrestrial. His symptoms are his antennae. His complexes are the organs that adapt him, not to life here, but to soul. His transference projections are phone calls to the Wordsworthian "imperial palace whence he came," or as Spielberg put it so nostalgically in his film: "E.T., phone home!"

The Body of Woody

The unnatural, or should I say 'sur-natural,' soul lives, moves and has its being less in the incarnational world of our arbi-trary life than in the imaginal world or constructed world man-kind has created for itself in the course of its human process. It is not in our incarnational anatomy of ten fingers and ten toes (and mostly two of everything else) that this soul dwells; the 'body' of the 'sur-natural' soul is the arts of the imagination. In poetry, painting, sculpture, architecture, dance, music, theater, etc., the sur-natural dimension of the soul finds the range, flexibility and extension necessary if it is to reach its full stature. Lear on the heath, the blinded Oedipus, Picasso's minotaur etchings, Duchamp's *Nude Descending a Staircase,* Stravinsky's "Firebird Suite," a video by the Rolling Stones, Spielberg's *E.T.,* Madonna's song "Like a Virgin" —every character in the world of art and entertainment together make up the support group of the sur-natural soul.

The function of theater, in Aristotle's view, is to provide emotional release to the audience—catharsis. A tragedy by Aeschylus, Sophocles or Euripides arouses in us feelings of pity and fear, develops them to a crescendo point, and absorbs the emotional discharge. From the naturalistic perspective all this is certainly true. Art can be used as vicariously as religion. But from a deeper, unnatural or 'sur-natural' perspective, it is not that our emotional tensions are being vicariously resolved by the wish-world of art; it is, rather, that the sur-natural soul is being released from its determinate fetters into the atmosphere of affirmed arbitrariness appropriate to it. The subtle body, the sur-natural soul, breathes fiction. It walks out of the silver screen and re-orders our contingent lives just as Mia Farrow's fictive lover walks out of the movie she is watching in Woody Allen's film *The Purple Rose of Cairo.* If we wish to understand this occult dimension of the so-called participatory emotions, it is to Allen, not Aristotle, that we will have to turn for guidance.

Fatality

Overwhelming events, events which cannot be incorporated into the life we have imagined for ourselves, cause the soul to bend back on itself, to commit "incest" with itself, and to revert to the heretical modes of the primary principle. Like the festering process which removes the sliver from a wound, the traumatized imagination works and re-works its metaphors until the events which have "pierced" it can be viewed in a more benign fashion. Paradoxically, the challenge posed for the soul by the vicissitudes of nature and the shocks of life must be resolved by a movement *against* nature and *against* life. Alchemy knew this aspect of the work of soul-making as the *opus contra naturam*, the work against nature into culture which nature herself desires.

In his book *An Outline of Psychoanalysis*, Freud defines the formation of the super-ego as a process based on the internalization of the external world: "A portion of the external world has, at least partially, been given up as an object and instead, by means of identification, taken into the ego—that is, has become an integral part of the internal world."[6] According to Freud, the ways in which the external world bumps, bruises and overwhelms us gradually become introjected and, in the normal course of events, come to discipline and rule the internal world. But when the external world has impinged upon the boundary of the body (primary narcissism) or upon the boundary of the ego (secondary narcissism) severely enough to cause a shock or trauma, it cannot be internalized and operate as the reality principle because the recipient container has been damaged in the process.

The last thing that a punctured, leaky, hystericized soul needs is more external "reality." Treatment aimed at adapta-

tion to normative models or internalization of the reality principle merely adds insult to injury. For, to the traumatized soul
the reality principle is a murdering parent, and this is something that cannot be cured through identification. The psychology of trauma, in other words, is the psychology of
personal fatality. Whenever a trauma is so deeply encoded on
the soul that it marks it as a fatality, our efforts to translate the
symptoms into prose will fail and our only recourse will be to
go on with them as poetry.

Nietzsche believed that if we are fool enough to affirm our
fatality we will become wise. His notions of the "convalescent
philosopher," "*amor fati,*" and "eternal recurrence" encour-
age the ontologization of the symptoms that constitute our
fate:

> My formula for greatness in a human being is *amor fati*:
> that one wants nothing other than it is, not in the future,
> not in the past, not in all eternity. Not merely to endure
> that which happens of necessity, still less to dissemble
> it—all idealism is untruthfulness in the face of necessity
> —but to *love* it. . . .[7]

Our personal fatality is the ink-well out of which we write
our personal mythology, our *amor fati,* our "yes" in the face
of necessity. Unable to conform to normative models, the
traumatized soul must invent its own until, as Keats wrote,
". . . branched thoughts, new grown with pleasant pain, instead
of pines shall murmur in the wind."[8]

The strange thing about the notion of normal development
and normative models is that they are essentially *static*.
They're fixed on the Aristotelian notion of growth as an
unfolding process or *entelechy* where the mature tree is from
the beginning contained in the tiny kernel. But life has never
enacted itself in such trauma-free laboratory conditions. In the
laboratory where processes enact themselves without having
to contend with the force of other influences, they can follow

in their father's footsteps. But outside the laboratory, life forms are constantly challenged, perturbed, and traumatized by external reality in ways they cannot internalize. In order to contend with this murdering paternal stimuli impinging on them, they must undergo evolutionary change, genetic drift, the creation of a personal mythology.

Therapy, when it does not respect the evolutionary character of fatality, risks placing patients in laboratory conditions, aborting their soul-making process and then giving up on them as contaminated samples. If the earliest forms of life on this planet had enacted themselves in trauma-free laboratory conditions, the complexity of life forms populating our present world would not have emerged. We would have followed in the father's footsteps and remained, like him, a single-celled organism.

This brings us to Jung's notion of incest. In Jung's view, those portions of the libido that cannot move forward into life to form what Freud would call realistic "object-cathexis" can re-order and cure themselves by regressing back into the maternal embrace of the collective unconscious. If the regressing libido is followed back to psychic layers "anterior to sexuality," the resultant "incest" will not be with the personal mother, which Freud rightly cautioned about, but with the Great Mother.

> The so-called Oedipus complex with its famous incest tendency changes at this level to a "Jonah-and-the-Whale" complex, which has any number of variants, for instance the witch who eats the children, the wolf, the ogre, the dragon, and so on. Fear of incest turns into fear of being devoured by the mother. The regressing libido apparently desexualizes itself by retreating back step by step to the presexual stage of earliest infancy. Even there it does not make a halt, but in a manner of speaking continues right back to the intra-uterine, pre-natal condition and, leaving

the sphere of personal psychology altogether, irrupts into the collective psyche where Jonah saw the "mysteries" ("representations collectives") in the whale's belly. The libido thus reaches a kind of inchoate condition in which, like Theseus and Peirithous on their journey to the under-world, it may easily stick fast. But it can also tear itself loose from the maternal embrace and return to the surface with new possibilities of life.[9]

When we cannot follow in the father's footsteps, when a trauma has erected a "do not enter" sign over the reality prin-ciple, we must regress to the mother's bed, dip our pens into the psychic gene pool of the collective unconscious, and return to the surface to write our personal mythology. The Oedipus-complex is the fatality of the traumatized soul, and as such it is less a complex to be resolved than a psychology to be affirmed.

When development is thwarted evolution begins. Whatever is turned back on itself by a trauma, whatever is forced to in-cestuously fertilize itself, is on the cutting edge of evolutionary change. The individuation process of the traumatized soul is less the unfolding development of the *a priori* coding of what it was always meant to be than it is a deviation or trans-mutation into something entirely new.

"You higher men," shrieks Nietzsche's Zarathustra, address-ing those who should have realized that their lives are a fatal-ity,

> Do you suppose I have come to set right what you have set wrong? Or that I have come to you that suffer to bed you more comfortably? Or to you that are restless, have gone astray or climbed astray, to show you new and easier paths?
>
> No! No! Three times no! Ever more, ever better ones of your kind shall perish—for it shall be ever worse and

harder for you. Thus alone—thus alone, man grows to the height where lightning strikes and breaks him: lofty enough for lightning.[10]

The End?

The compulsion to repeat, the compulsion to write yet another paragraph on trauma, is not stilled by this arbitrary ending. The problem of trauma can never be finally absorbed. Neither definitive textbooks nor approved gospels can be written. By their very nature traumas are individual and individuating. Like the grit in the oyster that occasions the pearl, overwhelming events stray into the substance of our lives and there start the festering process by which the soul is made.

Traumas are alien particles, just as a fleck of grit or a piece of sand are alien particles. When they lodge themselves in our lives, we are alienated from ourselves. Finding ourselves unable to absorb a trauma causes us to become a trauma to ourselves. The simple given-ness of our lives becomes extinct, and we must then begin a process of re-creating ourselves. It is in this way that trauma and alienation lead to soul-making.

The work on trauma is a repetition compulsion of ceaseless mental fight. Interminable analysis, interminable writing, interminable soul-making are the only medicine—there is no antidote. The transmuting of trauma into creative affirmations, the mutual transformation of trauma and soul, is a process that like poetry "survives in the valley of its saying" (Auden). To put it another way . . . and another way . . . and another way is what soul-making is all about.

Notes

Introduction

1. This holds true even when our references are to God-images drawn from biblical sources. While the believer may read the Bible to gain knowledge of the ontological God, the psychologist reads the Bible to gain knowledge of the soul. For him the Bible is a psychological document.

2. This sentence is not a logical deduction. I am *not* saying that since God is transcending and since trauma is transcending *therefore* God is a trauma. With the same reasoning, one could argue that since Africans and umbrellas are both black, Africans are umbrellas. My sentence is intended as a *description* of a *psychological identification* which exists between over-whelming events and the categories theology would reserve for deity. The psyche is irrational. It constantly makes deductions and ellipses which philosophy and theology would judge to be mistaken. But these identifica-tions are the *facts* of the psyche, regardless of their value to other disciplines. The psychologist's concern is with the brute fact that the traumatized soul is a theologizing soul—not with the merits of that resultant "theology" as theology.

3. This reading of Job presupposes Jung's reading in his "Answer to Job." The cat and mouse metaphor is his as well. This essay is included in volume 11 of C. G. Jung, *The Collected Works*, trans. R. F. C. Hull, ed. H. Read, M. Fordham, G. Adler, Wm. McGuire, Bollingen Series XX, vols. 1–20 (Princeton: Princeton University Press and London: Routledge and Kegan Paul, 1953 ff.). All further references to Jung's work will be by volume and paragraph numbers.

4. C. G. Jung, *CW* 11, ¶561.

5. James Hillman, *Re-Visioning Psychology* (New York: Harper & Row, 1975), p. 173.

6. Ibid., p. x.

7. C. G. Jung, *CW* 14, ¶603.

8. C. G. Jung, ibid., ¶781.

9. C. G. Jung, *CW* 13, ¶75.

10. Gary V. Hartman, "Psychotherapy: An Attempt At Definition," *Spring 1980*: 91.

11. William Wordsworth, "Lines Composed a Few Miles above Tintern Abbey," in *The Penguin Book of English Romantic Verse*, ed. David Wright (Harmondsworth: Penguin Books, 1968), p. 111.

12. C. G. Jung, *CW* 16, ¶390.

13. James Hillman, *Suicide and the Soul* (Dallas: Spring Publications, 1976), p. 23.

14. C. G. Jung, *CW* 11, ¶129.

15. Cf. James Hillman, *Re-Visioning Psychology*, pp. 95–99.

16. Sigmund Freud, "Further Recommendations in the Technique of Psycho-Analysis: Recollection, Repetition and Working Through," in *Collected Papers*, ed. Ernest Jones, trans. Joan Riviere, 5 vols. (London: Hogarth Press, 1950), 2: 370. All further references to the *Collected Papers* will be cited by volume and page numbers.

17. Ibid.

18. Ibid., p. 374.

19. Ibid., p. 373.

20. Cf. James Hillman, *Re-Visioning Psychology*, p. 18.

21. Cited by K. D. Newman in "Counter-Transference and Consciousness," *Spring 1980*: 117.

Chapter One

1. In John (15:1–2, 4–6) the meaning of suffering as punitive correction persists:

> I am the true vine, and My Father is the vine-dresser. Every branch in Me that does not bear fruit, He takes away; and every branch that bears fruit, He prunes it, that it may bear more fruit.... Abide in Me, and I in you. As the branch cannot bear fruit of itself, unless it abides in the vine, so neither can you, unless you abide in Me. I am the vine, you are the branches; he who abides in Me, and I in him, he bears much fruit; for apart from Me you can do nothing. If anyone does not abide in Me, he is

thrown away as a branch and dries up; and they gather them, and cast them into the fire, and they are burned.

2. Hans Kung, *On Being a Christian* (London: William Collins & Sons, 1978), p. 435.

3. Ibid., p. 434.

4. Ludwig Feuerbach, *Das Wesen des Christenthums* (Liepzig: Otto Wigand, 1883), p. 111.

5. Cited by Reidar Thomte in *Kierkegaard's Philosophy of Religion* (New York: Greenwood Press, 1969), p. 83.

6. Sören Kierkegaard, *Concluding Unscientific Postscript to the "Philosophical Fragments,"* trans. David F. Swenson, ed. Walter Lowrie (Princeton: Princeton University Press and American-Scandinavian Foundation, 1941), p. 432.

7. Cited by Walter Kaufmann in *Nietzsche: Philosopher, Psychologist, Antichrist* (New York: Vintage Books, 1968), p. 356.

8. James Hillman, *Re-Visioning Psychology*, p. 97.

9. Ibid., p. 95.

10. James Hillman [with Laura Pozzo], *Inter Views* (New York: Harper & Row, 1983), p. 76.

11. Ibid., p. 75.

12. A sentence of Jesus' from the Gospel of John (15 : 6) combines these two ideas and gives support to the view that the wrath of the Old Testament Father exists, as well, in the New Testament Son:

> If anyone does not abide in Me, he is thrown away [by God, the gardener] as a branch, and dries up; and they gather them, and cast them into the fire, and they are burned.

13. It may be objected at this point that God cannot be held responsible for the actions of those who act misguidedly in His name. Hillman has suggested, however, that every model structures its own uses and abuses and is thus responsible for both. It is not enough to say in hindsight that so and so was a bad Christian. God and Jesus, being the original models upon whom the behavior of the "bad believer" has been patterned, must not be exonerated from criticism. For Hillman's views about models and their shadows, see Louis Zinkin, "Is There Still a Place for the Medical Model," *Spring 1984*: 120.

14. Sigmund Freud and Joseph Breuer, "Early Studies on the Psychical Mechanism of Hysterical Phenomena," in *Collected Papers*, 5: 30.

15. C. S. Lewis, *The Problem of Pain* (London: William Collins & Sons, 1977), p. 4.

16. Ibid.

17. Ibid.

18. Ibid., p. 78.

19. Ibid.

20. Ibid.

21. C. G. Jung, *CW* 16, ¶257.

22. Sigmund Freud, *New Introductory Lectures on Psycho-Analysis* (Lecture 31), trans. W. J. H. Sprott (London: Hogarth Press, 1933), p. 78.

23. James Hillman, *Re-Visioning Psychology*, pp. 55–112.

24. Of course, in our lived life we do not make a distinction between primary and secondary narcissism. Often, patients who seem the most rigidly egoist are in fact the most severely traumatized on the level of primary narcissism. Ironically, it is amongst this population that we find the most devoted believers in the one true God who loves those who love him and keep his laws and punishes those who do not.

25. Lewis, *The Problem of Pain*, p. 83.

26. Ibid.

27. Ibid., pp. 83–84.

28. Ibid., p. 85.

29. Cited by Lyn Cowan in *Masochism: A Jungian View* (Dallas: Spring Publications, 1982), p. 21, from Norman Cohn, *The Pursuit of the Millennium* (New York: Oxford University Press, 1970), p. 128.

30. Cited by Lyn Cowan, ibid., p. 98, from Karen Horney, *New Ways in Psychoanalysis* (New York: W. W. Norton & Co., Inc., 1966), p. 248.

31. St. Theresa of Avila carefully distinguished the wish-fulfilling aspect of the imagination from a true vision of God: "It happens to some people ... that they become absorbed in their imagination to the extent that everything they think about seems to be clearly seen. Yet, if they were to see a real vision, they would know without any doubt whatsoever their mistake, for they themselves are composing what they see with their imagination." True vision, St. Theresa goes on to say, is entirely different from the wilful productions of the imagination: "In ... vision ... the soul is very far from thinking that anything will be seen, or having the thought even pass through its mind, suddenly the vision is represented to it all at once and stirs all the faculties and senses with a great fear and tumult so as to place them afterward in that happy peace." *The Interior Castle*, trans. Kieran Kavanaugh and Otilio Rodriguez (New York: Paulist Press, 1979), p. 158.

32. St. Theresa of Avila, *The Life of Saint Theresa of Avila by Herself*, trans. J.M. Cohen (London: Penguin Books, 1957), p. 210.

33. Evelyn Underhill, *Mysticism: A Study in the Nature and Development of Man's Spiritual Consciousness* (New York: E.P. Dutton & Co., 1961), p. 19.

34. A sentence of St. Paul's provides a scriptural basis for this behavior: "Therefore, since Christ has suffered in the flesh, arm yourselves also with the same purpose, because he who has suffered in the flesh has ceased from sin..." (1 Peter 4:1).

35. Cited by Evelyn Underhill in *Mysticism*, p. 218.

36. Rudolf Otto, *The Idea of the Holy*, trans. John W. Harvey (London: Oxford University Press, 1958), pp. 191–92.

37. Anonymous.

38. Friedrich Nietzsche, *The Portable Nietzsche*, ed. and trans. Walter Kaufmann (New York: The Viking Press, 1968), p. 197.

39. R.D. Laing, *The Divided Self* (New York: Pantheon Books, 1969), p. 94.

40. Ibid., p. 95.

41. C.G. Jung, *CW* 9, i, ¶195.

42. Nabíl, *The Dawn-Breakers: Nabíl's Narrative of the Early Days of the Bahá'í Revelation* (Wilmette, Il.: Bahá'í Publishing Trust, 1970), p. 293.

43. Ibid., p. 294.

44. Ibid., p. 411.

45. William Blake, *Selected Poetry and Prose of Blake*, ed. Northrop Frye (New York: Random House, 1953), p. 62.

Chapter Two

1. Willis Barnstone, ed., *The Other Bible* (New York: Harper & Row, 1984), p. 419.

2. Cited in Henri Corbin, "Divine Epiphany and Spiritual Birth in Ismailian Gnosis," in *Man and Transformation*, ed. J. Campbell, Papers from the Eranos Yearbooks, vol. 5, 2d ed. (Princeton: Princeton University Press, 1972), p. 69.

3. *The Other Bible*, p. 420.

4. Cited in Jeffrey Moussaieff Masson, *The Assault on Truth: Freud's Suppression of the Seduction Theory* (New York: Viking Penguin, 1985), pp. 108–09.

5. Cf. James Hillman, "Abandoning the Child," in *Loose Ends: Primary Papers in Archetypal Psychology* (Dallas: Spring Publications, 1975).

6. Cited by Masson, *The Assault on Truth*, pp. 117–18.

7. Milan Kundera, *The Unbearable Lightness of Being*, trans. Michael Henry Heim (New York: Harper & Row, 1985), pp. 6, 8.

8. Wallace Stevens, *The Palm at the End of the Mind*, ed. Holly Stevens (New York: Vintage Books, 1972), pp. 253-54.

9. John Keats, *Selected Poems and Letters*, ed. D. Bush (Boston: Houghton Mifflin, 1958), p. 288.

10. Cf. James Hillman, "Anima Mundi: The Return of the Soul to the World," *Spring 1982*: 80.

11. Cited by Rollo May, *Love and Will* (New York: Dell Publishing, 1969), p. 86.

12. Ibid., p. 85.

13. Samuel Taylor Coleridge, *Biographia Literaria*, ed. J. Shawcross, 2 vols. (Oxford: Oxford University Press, 1958), 1: 202.

14. For more on the image *of*/image *as* distinction, see James Hillman, "Further Notes on Images," *Spring 1978*: 173.

15. Friedrich Nietzsche, *The Philosophy of Nietzsche* (New York: The Modern Library, 1927), p. 11.

16. C. G. Jung, *CW* 12, ¶93.

Chapter Three

1. Sigmund Freud, *Beyond the Pleasure Principle*, ed. and trans. James Strachey (New York: W. W. Norton & Co., 1961), p. 30.

2. Ibid., pp. 32–33.

3. Ibid., p. 34.

4. Ibid.

5. Ibid., pp. 34–35.

6. Ibid., p. 20.

7. Ibid.

8. Ibid., p. 21.

9. Ibid., p. 26.

10. Friedrich Nietzsche, *Thus Spoke Zarathustra*, trans. R. J. Hollingdale (New York: Penguin Books, 1961), p. 69.

11. Freud, *Beyond the Pleasure Principle*, p. 26.

12. Ibid., p. 12.

13. Ibid., p. 21.

14. Ibid.

15. John Keats, *Selected Poems and Letters*, p. 288.

16. Sigmund Freud, *Beyond the Pleasure Principle*, p. 21.

17. Ibid., p. 25.

18. Ibid., p. 26.

19. Ibid., p. 35.

20. Friedrich Nietzsche, *Twilight of the Idols/The Anti-Christ*, trans. R.J. Hollingdale (Harmondsworth: Penguin Books, 1968), p. 117.

21. Ibid., p. 116.

Chapter Four

1. William Blake, *Selected Poetry and Prose of Blake*, p. 127.

2. Marie Fortune is a minister and the director of the Center for Prevention of Sexual and Domestic Violence in Seattle. She is the author of *Sexual Violence: The Unmentionable Sin*, a book which discusses sexual abuse and assault from a theological and pastoral perspective.

3. Counter-transference is an issue for the clergyperson no less than it is for the psychotherapist. Although "God" is spoken of in the approved manner characteristic of a particular denomination or faith, the clergyperson and believer may simultaneously use the term to propitiate events in the past, present, or future whose only claim to sacredness is that they have been, or threaten to be, traumatic.

4. Cited by John Bowlby, *Separation: Anxiety and Anger*, vol. 2 of *Attachment and Loss* (Harmondsworth: Penguin Books, 1975), p. 207.

5. Sigmund Freud, "Psycho-Analytic Notes upon an Autobiographical Account of a Case of Paranoia (Dementia Paranoides)," in *The Standard Edition of the Complete Psychological Works of Sigmund Freud*, ed. James Strachey, 24 vols. (London: Hogarth Press, 1953–74), 3: 448–49. All further references to *The Standard Edition* will be cited by volume and page numbers.

6. Ibid., p. 452.

7. W. G. Niederland, "Schreber: Father and Son," *Psychoanalytic Quarterly* 28 (1959): 151–69, and W. G. Niederland, "The 'Miracled-up' World of Schreber's Childhood," *Psychoanalytic Study of the Child* 14 (1959): 383–413.

8. Sigmund Freud, "Constructions in Analysis" (1937), in *The Standard Edition*, 5: 369.

9. Sigmund Freud, *Totem and Taboo and Other Works*, in *The Standard Edition*, 13: 144.

10. C. G. Jung, *Memories, Dreams, Reflections*, ed. Aniela Jaffé, trans. R. & C. Winston (New York: Random House, 1961), p. 39.

11. Sigmund Freud and C. G. Jung, *The Freud/Jung Letters: The Correspondence between Sigmund Freud and C. G. Jung*, ed. William McGuire, trans. Ralph Manheim and R. F. C. Hull (Princeton: Princeton University Press, 1974), p. 95.

12. Ibid.

13. "By 'archetype' I can refer only to the phenomenal archetype, that which manifests itself in images. The noumenal archetype per se cannot by definition be presented so that nothing whatsoever can be posited of it. In fact whatever one does say about the archetype per se is a conjecture already governed by an archetypal image. This means that the archetypal image precedes and determines the metaphysical hypothesis of a noumenal archetype." James Hillman, "On the Necessity of Abnormal Psychology," in *Facing the Gods* (Dallas: Spring Publications, 1980), p. 33.

14. James Hillman, "On the Necessity of Abnormal Psychology," *Eranos Jahrbuch 43—1974* (Leiden: E. J. Brill, 1977), p. 103.

15. Sigmund Freud, "On the Sexual Theories of Children," *Collected Papers*, 2: 69.

16. C. G. Jung, *CW* 14, ¶659.

Chapter Five

1. William Wordsworth, "Ode: Intimations of Immortality from Recollections of Early Childhood," in *The Penguin Book of English Romantic Verse*, p. 135.

2. Sigmund Freud and Joseph Breuer, "Early Studies on the Psychical Mechanism of Hysterical Phenomena," in *Collected Papers*, 5: 30.

3. William Wordsworth, "Ode: Intimations of Immortality," lines 80–85.

4. Ibid., p. 137.

5. Sigmund Freud, *New Introductory Lectures on Psycho-Analysis*, in *The Standard Edition*, 22: 80.

6. Sigmund Freud, *An Outline of Psychoanalysis*, trans. J. Strachey (London: Hogarth Press, 1949), p. 77.

7. Friedrich Nietzsche, *A Nietzsche Reader*, trans. R. J. Hollingdale (New York: Penguin Books, 1977), p. 260.

8. John Keats, "Ode to Psyche," in *The Penguin Book of English Romantic Verse*, p. 282, lines 52–53.

9. C. G. Jung, *CW* 5, ¶654.

10. Friedrich Nietzsche, *The Portable Nietzsche*, pp. 400–01.

Suffering and Polytheistic Imagination

Masochism: A Jungian View
Lyn Cowan
A radically new theory that regards masochism to be a manifestation of the "religious instinct." The author examines the symptoms of masochism and thoroughly discusses the clinical literature— Krafft-Ebing, Freud, and Jung. Combines precise clinical descriptions with a wealth of cultural and mythic evidence, and with special attention paid to masochism as an erotic and bodily path of individuation. (137 pp.)

Insearch: Psychology and Religion
James Hillman
Widely used in pastoral counseling and psychotherapeutic training, this book sets out the fundamental attitudes of Jungian psychology in a simple, yet deeply experiential style. Sensitively addresses such topics as listening, curiosity, confession, secrecy, befriending the dream, conscience, emotions and moods, problems of sexual love, and psychosomatics. (126 pp.)

Imagination is Reality
Roberts Avens
Places archetypal psychology within a major tradition of modern thought—mythical thinking—and recognizes imagination as the primal force and basic reality of human life. Drawing upon the writings of four twentieth-century thinkers, the author clarifies the post-Jungian direction of psycnology as it moves toward poetic and polytheistic imagination. He then compares the radical achievements of this direction in resolving the 'ego-question' with methods and ideas of the East: Buddhism, Tantrism, Zen, Vedanta. Bibliography. (127 pp.)

The New Polytheism
David L. Miller
With wit and a wealth of evidence, Miller presents the current return to polytheism in religion, psychology, sociology, and the arts, thereby challenging theology to re-imagine itself. "His notions are tantalizing," said *Time*. "A book you dare not miss," declared *Le Monde* in Paris. With a Preface by Henry Corbin and James Hillman's "Psychology: Monotheistic or Polytheistic" extensively revised. A provocative and perhaps prophetic book. Index. (148 pp.)

Spring Publications, Inc. • P.O. Box 222069 • Dallas, TX 75222